SpringerBriefs in Computer Science

T0253974

Series Editors

For further volumes:
http://www.springer.com/series/10028

Gregory O'Toole

Sustainable Web Ecosystem Design

 Springer

Gregory O'Toole
College of Information Sciences and Technology
Pennsylvania State University
University Park
PA
USA

ISSN 2191-5768   ISSN 2191-5776 (electronic)
ISBN 978-1-4614-7713-6   ISBN 978-1-4614-7714-3 (eBook)
DOI 10.1007/978-1-4614-7714-3
Springer New York Heidelberg Dordrecht London

Library of Congress Control Number: 2013939571

Printed on acid-free paper

Springer is part of Springer Science+Business Media (www.springer.com)

*Just as a torrent of burned Carbon atoms
into the air since the dawn of industrial man
has altered the fundamentals of the Earth's
atmosphere, a torrent of informational bits is
altering our sense of reality and what it
means to be a human being.*

Aristotelian format of the analogy is

*Carbon atoms : Atmosphere :: Information
bits : Reality*

This book is dedicated to the Gunthers, especially John, for the astounding record of human experience called "Death Be Not Proud," and Johnny and all of the other Glioblastoma multiforme patients and their families who have suffered. Your contribution to the understanding of the human ecosystem is invaluable. Also, to Morgan, Finnegan, "number 3", and my insightful wife, Carey

Preface

If you are reading this book you may or may not be aware that there is a virtual sea of instruction and help documentation freely available online to assist a beginner straight through to seasoned guru build and/or improve a Web site, Web app, or native mobile device app. To be clear, this book is *not* one of those documents. If you need to know how to optimize your site for beautiful, responsiveness in a mobile environment, how to resize a jpg, or how to secure your site from SQL injections, the help you need is out there on the Web and often times in many forms, but this book is not one of those forms. This book talks about those things briefly because they are certainly integral parts of the anatomy of the existing Web ecosystem. But this book does not explain those technologies or techniques. It simply addresses them as part of the larger informational context. This book is not a how-to manual in any way, unless you consider ideas about how these technologies fit together and act on each other and their users to be "how-to." Of course, there would be nothing wrong with that approach. In fact, often times, I take that approach myself. However, in brief, this book goes further in working to establish an early, comprehensive view of the basic, important nodes of Web interface development within the greater context of real world human–computer interaction issues.

In this current beta release, this book's primary role is as a companion text to the IST250 course offered by the College of Information Sciences and Technology at The Pennsylvania State University, however, you certainly do not need to be enrolled in the class in order to find value in the book's message. The technologies mentioned above, along with many others, are the technical basis of a basic Web instance and are covered thoroughly in IST250 during the semester. This book does not duplicate that course material as much as it points to those technologies and illustrates how they work together, and work with us, the users. The roles that these technologies now play in our lives cause bigger questions to arise. This book is concerned with those questions. In *Image, Meaning, Text*, Roland Barthes points out the difference between a *denoted* message and a *connoted* message. Barthes showed us that when a photograph is shown to a viewer there is a signifier involved from which the viewer finds the signified, that is, the denoted message, the plain message, the simple message, the message that is contained within the image alone. In other words, when a person looks at a photograph, they may find some meaning there. When the same person looks at the same photograph, but this time the image is within a context, that is, a newspaper page, for example, with a headline, a caption, story text, and maybe even an advertisement or two or three running adjacent to the image, a different meaning may come about for the viewer than when the image was seen on its own. This is what Barthes termed the connoted message. In our rich information landscape, connoted messages are everywhere. They are all over the Web causing high beta brain waves, waves associated with decision-making and high mental simulation. This is the condition of our world today and, for good or ill, it is only going to increase. So, we must be aware of it and do our best to understand it.

It is the aim of this book to broaden your view of what the Web really is. The hope is that perhaps in a slightly less immediate kind of way, this book will help you build, or at least contribute to, a better Web ecosystem. This book is just as important to shaping a healthy future as it is about what you can to right now toward that goal. If you are interested in taking part in the progression of a sustainable Web ecosystem, then please read on to find out how to become an active participant.

Acknowledgments

A special thank you is deserved to all of the hard working people involved in the Web communities at The Pennsylvania State University, The Art Institute of Pittsburgh Online Division, and the European Graduate School. Thanks to the countless independent artists, writers, technicians, project managers, engineers, and programmers I have worked with over the past 20 years. This book would not have been possible without the time I put in working with many excellent people at Sunoco, Inc., the University of Denver, Baker College, ITT, NIIT, Bradley University, The School of the Art Institute of Chicago, and, of course, the *Missoulian* way up in big sky Missoula, Montana. Thank you.

With permission minor parts of this book have been revised based on partial IST250 course content offered by the College of Information Sciences and Technology (IST) at The Pennsylvania State University. Brett Bixler, Mike Halm, Gerry Santoro, Fred Aebli, and Sue Monk contributed the course content.

Contents

1 Introduction: Discovering Where We Are Not 1

2 Seeing Where We Need to Be 7
   2.1 The Anatomy of Sustainable Web Ecosystem Design 9

3 Getting There: Landing an Onion on Mars 11

4 The Necessity of a Sustainable Web Ecosystem 15
   4.1 Individual, Medium, Society 17

5 The Real Discovery: The Web is Glial 19

6 Web User Research 25
   6.1 HCI/BCI 26
   6.2 Surveys 30
   6.3 Usability 30
   6.4 Focus Groups 31
   6.5 Web User Profiles 31

7 The Project 33
   7.1 Vision 33
   7.2 Brand/Message 34
   7.3 Communication 34
   7.4 Balanced Media Ecosystem 35

8 Project Management 37
   8.1 Pre-production 37
      8.1.1 Concept Document/Functional Specification 37
      8.1.2 Competitive Matrix 41
      8.1.3 Cost Benefit Analysis 41

8.2   Team Roles and Methods 42
        8.2.1   Development Team Roles and Responsibilities..... 42
8.3   Source Code Management 43
8.4   Development Journal............................ 43

9   Architecture.................................... 45
9.1   Web Content Management Systems 45
9.2   Taxonomy 46
9.3   Intuitive Tagging 47
9.4   SEO Optimization.............................. 47

10   Functionality 49
10.1   Hypertext..................................... 49
10.2   Hypertext Transfer Protocol....................... 50
10.3   HyperText Markup Language (HTML) 50
10.4   Document Object Model 51
10.5   Web Browsers 51
        10.5.1   Background 52
        10.5.2   Popular Web Browser Descriptions............ 53
10.6   Accessibility................................... 54
        10.6.1   The Limitations of the Users' Computer Systems ... 54
        10.6.2   The Limitations of the User................. 55
10.7   Universality 56
10.8   Searchability 56
10.9   Scalability 57
10.10   Social-Sharing 57
10.11   Responsiveness................................. 57
10.12   Testing 58

11   Image.. 59
11.1   Data Visualization 59
11.2   Multi-Formats 59
        11.2.1   Definitions of Basic Terms 60
11.3   Dynamic Interface 61
11.4   Image Genome................................. 63

12   Writing 65
12.1   Creative...................................... 65
12.2   Technical..................................... 65
12.3   Documentary 66
12.4   Critical 66

13   Code   67
    13.1   Stability Through Standards   67
    13.2   Lightweight   68
    13.3   Secure   69
    13.4   Open   69
             13.4.1   Semantic   70
    13.5   Interoperable   71
    13.6   Energy Utilization   72

14   Web Hosting   73
    14.1   Efficiency   75
    14.2   Performance   75
    14.3   Lightweight Stability   76
    14.4   Reconciling Project and Host   77
             14.4.1   Content Considerations   78
             14.4.2   Image Slices   79
             14.4.3   Measuring Performance   79
    14.5   Security   80
             14.5.1   Types of Security   81
             14.5.2   Web Security   82
             14.5.3   Site Design   82
             14.5.4   Site Development   83
             14.5.5   Site Management   83
             14.5.6   User Considerations   84

15   Post Launch   85
    15.1   Maintenance   85
    15.2   Workflow   85
    15.3   Content Provider Groups, (e)Teaching, (e)Learning   86
    15.4   User Groups, Community   87
    15.5   Analytics   88

16   Education   91

17   Policy   95
    17.1   Web Standards: The W3C   96
    17.2   Freedom of Speech/Human Rights   97
    17.3   Politics   97
    17.4   Health   98
    17.5   Economics   98
    17.6   Open Accessibility   99
    17.7   Environment   99
    17.8   Education 100

18   Philosophy of Technology 101
      18.1   Fredrick Jameson 101
      18.2   Jean Francois Lyotard 103
      18.3   Harold Innis 106
      18.4   Emile Durkheim 109

19   Conclusion 111

Book Editions/Versioning Information 113

References 115

Chapter 1
Introduction: Discovering Where We Are Not

Today there is an increasingly important and relevant space between the core of the networked computer and the brain (or mind) of the user. If you replicate that area about 2.3 billion times, you have not only a pretty serious condition, but also a fairly rough sketch of our existence today. That is, 33 % of the planet's human population is connected to and utilizes the Web. In 2013, about a billion people will do this actively, while using the Web from a mobile device ("Internet World Stats"). That is why this book exists. It is a survey of the activity in this area and some discussion about why these topics are significant to humans. In a nutshell, the ways in which we go about building parts of the Web directly affect the larger context of the Web. Web sites have become increasingly dense. As more and more services and information are made available over the Internet and intranets, Web sites have become extraordinarily complex, while their correctness is often crucial to the success of businesses, governments, and our social relations (Benedikt, Freire, and Patrice). It is becoming more and more apparent as time goes on that the context of the Web is the context for a large part of humanity. Not so trivial topics such as keeping the Web open for freedom of speech, and simultaneously protecting our youth from pornography and cyber bullying; allowing for the Web to be effective for government, but policed of the abuse of power and political terrorism; and making sure that the Web is a medically, physiologically, and emotionally healthy environment for individuals and society. These are lofty goals, and achieving them starts with the smaller decisions Web developers, designers, stake holders, admins, and users make every time they access their devices.

This book and the ideas it contains come as a result of working for nearly twenty years in the field of semiotics, that is, the study of signs, and expressive media communication technology. Believe it or not, I didn't fully realize I was working in semiotics until well into that time period. Some times we come to things along very different paths from one another. I started out studying visual communication in the form of photojournalism at Bradley University in the early 1990s. When I graduated with a B.S. degree in 1995 I had two years of manual, chemical, and dark room photography, and one year of Adobe Photoshop (without a version number yet) and Netscape Navigator under my belt. I had an Apple

G. O'Toole, *Sustainable Web Ecosystem Design*,
SpringerBriefs in Computer Science, DOI: 10.1007/978-1-4614-7714-3_1,
© The Author(s) 2013

PowerBook 100, a brick-like laptop computer with a trackball and a gray scale monitor. A year later I upgraded to a Mac PowerBook 165c—Apple's first laptop with a color screen.

A short while later in Wicker Park in Chicago I began working seriously as a fine art painter, first in acrylic then in oil. I showed my work in galleries in Chicago, the Chelsea District in New York City, and in Kotka, Finland (not to mention anywhere else in between that would hang my paintings on the walls). For a decent paycheck I started putting my Photoshop skills to work in and around the Chicago Loop creating clipping paths and retail magazine catalog compositions for advertising and production companies servicing colossal clients like Meier, Home Depot, and Sears. I branched out when I enrolled for a Post-Baccalaureate degree at The School of the Art Institute of Chicago to take still life oil painting classes and ended up falling in love with two new lifelong companions called HTML (hypertext markup language) and CSS (Cascading Style Sheets). I put them to work right away in any way that I could. I quickly moved on to troubleshooting Javascript errors and adding browser functionality for Harpo Studios in the West Loop a.k.a. the Website for the *Oprah Winfrey Show.*

Being an adventurous, recalcitrant twenty-something, before long I packed some camping gear and the laptop into my 1995 Ford Ranger™ and headed out for the Rocky Mountains where I quickly landed the job of Art Director for *Aspen Magazine.* We put out a 250-page holiday issue with a commission by artist Ralph Steadman on the cover. Part of the job was working with ads still in film format from clients like Rolex™, Calvin Klein™, Land Rover™, and The North Face™. From time to time the editor compensated good work with new K2 skis. Life was fun in the Roaring Fork Valley, but I didn't stay in one place for too long.

I worked as an editorial and Web content designer for the *Telluride Daily Planet* in Telluride, Colorado and got entrance to the legendary Telluride Bluegrass Festival. Then I worked as graphic designer building ads for the *Missoulian* in Missoula, Montana. Later I worked as a photojournalist and enviro-political op-ed columnist for the *Bigfork Eagle*, *Whitefish Pilot* and the *Daily Inter Lake* on the far western edges of Glacier National Park in Montana where I lived in a log cabin along the Swan River and often times in the dead of winter would not see another human for days. I wrote and published books of poems and individual short stories about my travels and my life and accepted a grant from the Montana Arts Council and the National Endowment for the Arts. I was not satisfied.

I enrolled in the Digital Media Studies (DMS) program at the University of Denver in 2003 to pursue the Master of Arts degree because I wanted a solo exhibition in a major gallery. I had been told by some of the big River North district curators in Chicago that most of the galleries in that neighborhood won't even look at an artist's portfolio unless they have a graduate degree, usually the terminal MFA. I figured the MA might help, but there was something else pulling me toward this cross-disciplinary field of study. When I arrived in Denver for orientation and introduced myself to one of the faculty members who had been on the selection committee for accepting new graduate students he looked at me, paused, and said this: "Oh, you're that poet."

It's all related. The work I've done stands out in different ways to different people. People see what they are interested in. People see what they want to see. This has become clear to me in the years since.

I continued to paint, take photographs, and experiment with mixed, digital media to create new types of art in the Mile High City. I covered culture and technology related events on campus and wrote articles about them for the *Clarion*, the University of Denver newspaper. In the classroom I discovered media philosophy and critical theory and realized the wealth of wisdom that could be extracted from thinkers like Adorno, Horkheimer, and the rest of the Frankfurt School, Friedrich Kittler and Jean Baudrillard. Before Denver the deepest I went was Kerouac and Richard Brautigan. I was right where I needed to be.

I got more and more work in Web design and was asked by the Dean of DMS to serve as the Teaching Assistant for his introductory level HTML course. Also that year I took a class in Adobe Coldfusion Web application development and fell in love all over again. I was officially addicted to relational databases that I could connect to fluid and fluent, beautiful Web-based digital interfaces. It was the perfect merger of art, technology and human-viewer psychology that I had been looking for whether I had fully recognized it or not.

There is a fine arts counterpart to DMS at DU called the Electronic Media Arts and Design program (eMAD). Early one spring in Denver I was asked by one of the eMAD faculty to teach his Net Art class while he was in South America on sabbatical. I accepted, of course, and never looked back. I put the design and development skills to use as the Web designer for DU's Sturm College of Law and other units around campus. I graduated, left DU and went to work for private Web shops in Lower Downtown Denver where the pay was double.

I applied one day to teach a Web class online at a small Colorado college and they ended up offering me the job of Assistant Program Director for their Web Design and Game Art program. I took it. It turned out that I didn't like the administration role, but I loved teaching Web topics online. I left the job but continued teaching in the online classroom.

I applied and was accepted to the Ph.D. program in Media and Communication at the European Graduate School in Saas-fee, Switzerland where I attended intensive resident sessions discussing media and communication theory and Continental philosophy in classrooms perched just below the 15,000 foot high Dom Mountain in the peaks of the craggy, glaciated, and snow-capped Swiss Alps. I completed work on my doctoral dissertation which is an ambitious attempt to tacked at least part of the problem that is the contemporary state of extracting meaning from mediated messages. The ideas of French philosopher Jean-Francois Lyotard, Canadian Harold Innis, and others heavily influence the analysis.

I wrote instructional documentation for innovative online services being upstarted by Sears Holdings Corporation at their corporate headquarters in Hoffman Estates, Illinois. I wrote online Web and digital media college level courses for NIIT in India and served as Subject Matter Expert (SME) for ITT Technical Institute in the U.S. I taught online Web design classes for the Graduate Program at Baker College in Flint, Michigan. I started teaching as an Adjunct for

The Art Institute of Pittsburgh Online Division in the Department of Web Design and Interactive Media, and soon was offered a Full Time Faculty position where I was offered the Teaching Excellence Award the following year.

In Philadelphia I worked with the environmental engineers as a technical writer and interface specialist for Sunoco's Health, Environment and Safety Division at the Mellon Bank Building in Center City and at the refineries in Marcus Hook. I enjoyed a healthy respect in this role and felt like I was contributing something important to something important. I was on contract and I would have pursued a long career doing this type of work for the company, but the economic downslide of 2008 caused hiring freezes at the corporate level. I moved on, applied, interviewed, and landed at The Pennsylvania State University 190 miles west in State College, PA, converting legacy, static html web sites to dynamic, open source content management environments like Plone and Drupal.

Not long after arriving in Nittany Valley I was offered to teach a class called Introduction to Photography as an adjunct faculty member in the College of Arts and Architecture. My day job was working as the one-man Web department in the Social Science Research Institute when I started a biomedical Human Computer Interaction (or Brain Computer Interaction) research project with the neurology department at St. Alexis Medical Center in Hoffman Estates, Illinois measuring comparative brain wave activity of humans while consuming different types of media including codex books, Web sites, handheld mobiles, and e-ink devices like the Barnes & Noble Nook® and the Sony Reader®. We monitored electroencephalography (EEG) during media consumption and, needless to say, have some very interesting results.

After three years on staff doing Web management, design and development at Penn State I was promoted to a faculty member at the College of Information Sciences and Technology (IST) where I teach Introduction to Web Design and Development and work with Plone and Drupal as the Senior Web Designer and Web Initiative Committee Chair.

I elucidate on this rather long story full of details because it is exactly this professional path that I've taken, and the evolution of the media communication technologies involved that are the reasons that this book exists. This book needed to be written to show how all of this and much, much more goes into engineering and understanding a successful, sustainable, usable Web system. There are so many moving parts and important, relevant nodes to map out as parts of the anatomy of sustainable Web ecosystem design that it takes a book to do it. Of course, we could make a long, mundane, bulleted list, but that would not be nearly as much fun.

I am not a system administrator, nor have I ever worked as one. But I have worked alongside plenty and have done so long enough to appreciate the complexity of their role. I am not a hardcore programmer or an expert in object-oriented programming, but I have respected experts in my circles. If I didn't I wouldn't get very far. I am not a system security expert, but they play an important role here as well making sure the environments I create are as stable as possible from disaster, intentional or otherwise. I never even knew "business analyst" was a specialty in information technology until I worked alongside several people with this job title programmatically matching the interface functionality of an online environment to the business services offered by the company. It was a fascinating puzzle to solve. In other words, to build a sustainable Web ecosystem that can harmoniously exist in today's world and one that has what it takes to remain relevant five years from now, it takes the proverbial village. You get the idea.

When we break it down in such a way it starts to become very clear how many moving parts we have to consider, plan, design, develop, manage, and sustain. It is a complex system that doesn't end with the machines we use. The human developers, designers, testers, and users are part of it as well. In fact, the distance between human and computer is minute if it exists at all. Even the stakeholders are a part of this system because, for starters, they influence decision making all along the way. Thus, we have ecosystems. A more accurate way of putting it would be to say that we have one vast ecosystem into which we are plugging the smaller ecosystems that we build. And as we all know well, if an ecosystem is not sustainable then it is not much good to us over time.

This book is a contribution to the important and, thankfully, ongoing discussion of our information world and how we, as players in that world, engage, interact, and sustain in healthy and productive ways. It considers, perhaps not exhaustively, the many and varied components that make up the anatomy of a professional and competently built sustainable Web ecosystem.

Chapter 2
Seeing Where We Need to Be

Information is everything and everything is information. As world renowned physicist John Archibald Wheeler poetically puts it: "it from bit," meaning every "it," that is, "every particle, every field of force, even the space-time continuum itself, derives its way of action and its very existence entirely, even if in some contexts indirectly, from the detector-elicited answers to yes or no questions, binary choices, bits." What Wheeler means here is that "all things physical, all *its*, must in the end submit to an information-theoretic description" (Wheeler). In other words: everything is information. It is not easy to put the ideas of this book, that is, the ideas describing the anatomy of sustainable Web ecosystem design, into a neat and clean box. In fact, I am not sure it is even possible. We know that this is the case because what we are really talking about here is organizing, indexing, and making it fun and efficient to access information. As we know, information is everything, everywhere, all of the time. At this point in human evolution it is not unlike a fish trying to understand water. Quite frankly, that is a tough idea to get your head around. Further, we are not simply trying to understand that information is everything, everywhere, but we are trying to go a step further and become information's master manipulator. At will, no less. Then put it onto devices, many different kinds of devices, and make it accessible to billions of people across countries, languages, ages, backgrounds and abilities. We want to make information work well for us. We want to make it sustainable over time. In all, what we face is no small task. That is why this book has been written. Essentially what we are talking about is a unified theory on how to create the interface between front end Web design and development methodologies and practices matched with the every day human user. This is a tall order.

In our current media-rich environment a Web site is more than a collection of relative html documents containing text and other digital media that are stored on a static server in a file system waiting to be served up to a singular desktop computer monitor. Early on, in fact, this was the case, however, those days are long gone. In the 20 years since Netscape Navigator invaded private homes and played a major role in bringing the Internet to the masses we reached a point where there are an unlimited number of possible combinations of screens, devices, platforms,

G. O'Toole, *Sustainable Web Ecosystem Design*,
SpringerBriefs in Computer Science, DOI: 10.1007/978-1-4614-7714-3_2,
© The Author(s) 2013

browsers, locations, versions, users, uses, and Exabytes of all types of data with which those of us on the connected side of the access digital divide can interact. This is complicated. Further, today our mediated atmosphere surrounds us all of the time, and in nearly every place. It is an information-centric ecosystem that is part human, part hardware, and part software. A unique condition is upon us. This book is about a methodology of creating Web-based systems (i.e. Web sites, mobile environments, content, etc.) that considers each of the parts, the modules, the organisms—binary or otherwise—that constitute the anatomy of a balanced, sustainable Web ecosystem. Written in a highly approachable, practical style in hopes of making a complex condition easily accessible the messages contained in this book are useful for stakeholders, system administrators, developers, designers, content managers, and the anonymous Web user in industry and the same plus faculty, staff, and students of all levels involved in teaching and learning in information technology.

This book aims at describing a theory of each of the requisite nodes that must come together and function in a type of harmony in order to create a sustainable informational system in general, and one that includes Web functionality and user interface interactivity in particular. The whole system that is the Web presence— that is, a sum of all of the required parts, elements, steps, and considerations that are part of the recipe—needs to be designed for sustainability. This is not solely a political debate. It is not only an economic strategy. It is not an autonomous ethically-eco decision concerning our information and technological health. It is all of these. And here, as in other sustainability-driven initiatives, the real value resides in the sum total.

As anyone who has been involved in creating a Web-based system knows it is an understatement to say that there are a lot of moving parts to this process. The planning, design, development, even the users can and do change often. Heck, even the environment itself where a project is taking place can change. What makes the process more complex still is that the parts don't stop moving once the goal has been achieved. The parts are always moving, no matter what stage in the design and development process you are in. To add yet another layer of complexity to the process, the future of the technology we are using to build today as well as the environments in which this technology will (hopefully) be working in the future are also somewhat uncertain. We strive for the best possible outcomes in a nearly perfectly dynamic environment, using tools and methods that are equally dynamic in nature. It is for precisely this reason that this book exists. It is a book of one idea made up of many different parts. That one idea is a theory, a methodology, of what needs to be considered and taken into account when creating an informational Web system of any kind. No matter what you are dreaming, scheming, planning, designing, developing or maintaining, these are considerations that need to be made. Whether you are working in industry, ecommerce, education, politics, or as a fine artist creating and/or publishing your work, these considerations need to be made. This book is not a coding how-to manual. This is not a resource to learn how to get your hosting servers up and running, or how to update and patch your content management systems for security. This is not even a book on how to design a beautiful Web or mobile interface. There are countless resources in the world today for these topics—some of them are even pretty good. This book is about a fresh, holistic perspective on how to bring a rather long set of important processes together, that is, to be thoughtful in order to create the most lightweight, accessible, exciting, and sustainable Web ecosystem. Consider it a mile-high view, but an important view to be certain.

2.1 The Anatomy of Sustainable Web Ecosystem Design

The necessary nodes of the front end Web-human interface ecosystem are referred to as the anatomy, which is simply a dissection of the whole system. Here we look at the important parts of that whole. In order to illustrate this anatomy of the ecosystem we can use this infographic in Fig. 2.1. The infographic shows the relationships that are created from each of the important considerations in the Web ecosystem. To address and understand each of these areas as you embark on your next Web project means that you are in a sound place. You are off on the right foot,

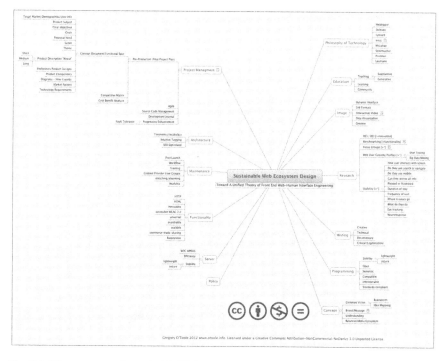

Fig. 2.1 The anatomy of sustainable Web ecosystem design shows the necessary nodes of the ecosystem, the dissection of the whole. This node map is updated frequently. A high resolution, updated version of this infographic is freely available at http://www.otoole.info

so to speak, and you will have a strong start to your project, and a road map that will aid in the successful achievement of your goals.

Please note that this freely available infographic is maintained online at http://www.otoole.info. Visit the site at any time to zoom in and get a closer look at the anatomy. The online version is also updated periodically and therefore you will be able to view the most recent version. Further, the online version includes the context of how the anatomy of sustainable Web ecosystem design fits into the relationship schema of the individual, information, and society. This topic is introduced later in this book.

Suggested Web Resource(s):

Anatomy of Sustainable Web Ecosystem Design infographic: http://www.otoole.info.

Chapter 3
Getting There: Landing an Onion on Mars

To try to simplify the ideas in this book it is helpful to visualize this informational ecosystem in layers. To aid in this one might imagine a metaphor to describe the involved dynamic and continuous process. It is somewhat of a two-part metaphor to be specific. The first part is the layered onion: a common enough metaphor and therefor an effective metaphor. The second part is the difficulty involved in the process of flying a spacecraft to places beyond the earth's atmosphere. Landing an onion on Mars, of course, has a certain element of humor and jest to it, but it works. As a two-part metaphor it makes sense because when we are working with building a Web ecosystem we are first working with the apparatus, that is, the desktop, laptop, or mobile device that will be used to build and operate the product we are working to construct. This is our onion. The modern computer and everything it does functions in a way that we can think about in layers: there is a lot going on around the surface, but what happens here is a result of deeper layers that are doing an important amount of work.

Aside from all of the hardware and electricity, most of what allows a computer to function, that is, to communicate with itself and ultimately other computers is code. At the very center of the onion a computer's central processing unit functions with what we call machine code. This is the binary system of symbols made up of strings of 1's and 0's organized in sets of 8 that humans have a tough time making sense of. This works well for the machine because it is binary, relatively lightweight and efficient.

On top of the machine code, the next layer of the onion's skin is called the assembly language. This is the computer language that humans can read, write, and make sense of which communicates with the computer's machine code that is located one layer lower. The assembly languages communicate with the machine code often using compilers and linkers depending on the type of language. The assembly language in turn works with other programming languages such as C for example to create what we call the lower-level languages. These layers form a sort of nerve center of the computational device. There is a lot of interaction going on between human and computer but it is often times in the form of programming.

G. O'Toole, *Sustainable Web Ecosystem Design*,
SpringerBriefs in Computer Science, DOI: 10.1007/978-1-4614-7714-3_3,
© The Author(s) 2013

The next layer of the onion comes in the form of what are called higher-level languages. Largely it is in this higher-level that we can program and build applications with which the users of our products can interact in an uncountable number of ways. It is in this higher-level language layer that we find common computer programming languages such as C++, Objective-C, Java, C#, VB.NET, Ruby, Python, PHP, Javascript and ActionScript. These are called object-oriented languages and they tend to be relied on for the heavy lifting that may need to be included in an interactive environment. Interactive design and development usually includes relational or other types of databases that store the information a user is interacting with. At this level it is important to consider how the programs will interact with and use raw and formatted data.

Further out we have another layer to the onion that includes lighter-weight languages. Many of the languages in this layer are called markup languages. Markup languages, such as HTML5, XML, and CFML are used mainly for structure, communication, and display of data. HTML, the hypertext markup language, is the standard for pages on the World Wide Web. For our purposes, we can consider the standard Web styling language called Cascading Style Sheets (CSS) to be included in this layer of the computer-based Web system. When considering a Web site or a native mobile app, this layer plays a major role in the user interface engineering of the product. None of the layers really ever does much on their own. These layers continually work together to make happen what we tell the computer to do.

If the computer or mobile device is our metaphorical onion, than it is possible that this is where it ends. However, for purposes of continuing the illustration, we may consider the next layer out to be where we start to see the humans interacting with the computer that is running the product we built. This is the complexity of an ecosystem: where does one node of the system start and another one end? The important thing here is to see and understand these layers of our mobile, computing vegetation.

Talking about the layers of an onion is simply one way of understanding the layers of a computing system and the environment that surrounds it. This would stay a fairly simple condition if we built computers today, understood them fully, and kept the same computing devices forever. However, for good or ill, this is not the case. This is where the second part of our two-part metaphor (landing an onion on Mars) becomes relevant. Due to the uncertainty and open-endedness of digital media information technology, the complexity involved in creating and maintaining a successful informational Web system or product, and the rapid rate of evolution of the technology and processes involved, creating a sustainable Web ecosystem is a lot like NASA sending the Curiosity Rover to Mars (and almost as exciting). What we are working on today is a product that will eventually go into the unknown. Rover engineers don't know all of the variables in the Mars operation just like we don't know what new media communication and information technologies are just over the horizon. What we build today must be based on our reliable understanding of the immediate. In the world of the Web this is difficult enough. We must understand and consider each of these nodes for every project we take on. But this is not all. All the while we also must keep in mind that what we are building needs not only to survive, but also needs to be useful to us once it launches and is put to use "out there".

It is with a clear understanding of these multi-layered challenges that we are in the best position to be well prepared as we set of to construct lightweight, scalable, accessible, mobile, usable, creative Web systems. It is a fun and complicated process, but when it is done properly, can create a small piece of a better world that can be useful for years to come.

Chapter 4
The Necessity of a Sustainable Web Ecosystem

Beyond the practical Web design and development applications of the sustainable Web ecosystem model there are certainly many higher-level applications. Every day those of us on this side of the access digital divide see the change and effect that the Internet has conducted on just about everything. Our classrooms, places of work, modes of business, social spots, electoral processes, sporting events, theaters, museums, parks, historic markers, methods of politics—essentially almost every way in which we interact with the world around us—have all been substantially impacted and altered in the past few years by the Web.

The increased complexity that we are involved with here can be quantitatively explored using a time and technology based thought experiment. Take a look at this thought experiment as in Table 4.1. This experiment looks at a likely media and communication scenario for a person working in an office environment today. The thought exercise counts up the number of possible or likely interactions a professional in any given time period might be dealing with at any given time during their workday. This is similar to the idea of multitasking concerning media communication technology. The historic time periods listed in Table 4.1 are established by the advent of these important technologies and their use in the professional environment. Each of the criteria is explained in more detail here.

To clarify, the first current historic time period in the exercise stands for the contemporary period, largely consisting of the past two decades or less, when the Internet was a standard piece of professional communication technology. The second historic time period in Table 4.1 is the period of professional human activity before the Web was prevalent as it is in the first time period, but after the advent and during common use of the typewriter. The third historic time period pertains to the time period before the telephone was in common, everyday use in the professional setting. The fourth time period is significant of the time before the mechanical typewriter was in use. The fifth historic time span show in the exercise exemplifies the period before the widespread use of the printing press with moveable type. The sixth period is significant of the time span before man commonly used the written word, when most human communication was done through spoken word, graphics, and other non-literary means. Finally, the seventh historic

G. O'Toole, *Sustainable Web Ecosystem Design*,
SpringerBriefs in Computer Science, DOI: 10.1007/978-1-4614-7714-3_4,
© The Author(s) 2013

Table 4.1 A thought experiment for media use. This thought experiment quantifies a likely media and communication scenario for a person working in an office environment

Historic time period	Internet/ Typewriter	Telephone	Desk/ "Place"	Person	Total
1. Current	5+	2+	2	1	10+
2. Before Web w/typewriter	1	1	2	1	5
3. Before telephone	1	0	2	1	4
4. Before typewriter	0	0	2	1	3
5. Before printing press (w/written word)	0	0	2	1	3
6. Before written word	0	0	1	1	2
7. Before spoken word	0	0	1	0	1

time period shown in this thought experiment is the oldest time span and is significant of the time before humans commonly had established, spoken language at their disposal.

The comparative exercise criteria across the top of Table 4.1 pertain to the media technologies that have dominated human communication in the professional environment over the past several thousand years. The descriptor "Internet/ Typewriter" is signifies common use of the mechanical or electronic typewriter or the Internet for emailing and other Web based operations to communicate with coworkers, customers, clients and so forth. This category is significant for any typewriter or Web technologies predominantly used to complete tasks at work. The two technologies are included in the same column due to the fact that the personal computer largely replaced the typewriter over time. The "Telephone" descriptor signifies common use of the telephone to communicate and complete tasks at work. The "Desk" descriptor signifies the use or consumption of physical papers, forms, newspapers, and all other paperwork on the worker's desk as a way of completing tasks at work or gaining news and other required information in order to do one's job. Of course, if we look back across time far enough we know that before a certain time period humans did not use desks for work. In this case, the descriptor "Desk" means something similar to "Place of work" to signify activities that would have been required of the worker at the time such as making tools, hunting and gathering, farming, or cooking meals to survive. The "Person" descriptor signifies another physical human being (i.e. coworker, colleague, manager, etc.) walking by or otherwise physically arriving in the presence of the worker, usually talking or using other (body) language-based communication to interact with the worker. A coworker stopping by the worker's desk in person to talk and discuss tasks at work or scheduled meetings are examples of the "Person" descriptor.

Looking at the total columns here it is clear how much more activity going on there is for the professional office worker today. This thought experiment could be used in any working environment in any country in the world and we may see interesting results. It is certainly true in industrial and information dominated economies across the globe. The most significant change here is in the transition from pre-Web times to our current Internet dominated condition. This is clearly illustrated in this thought experiment.

In some ways, it is quite easy to see that the Web is a type of step in our human evolution. We see it clearly here in our professional context. Perhaps this is only semantics and not biology, but it doesn't matter, the shift the world is experiencing due to the easy transmission and access to information is significant.

This step in our evolution is remarkably different than those of the past because this time we have some control over what is happening. We have the abilities to steer these changes in the right directions toward the goals of universal benefit. Among others, a sustainable Web ecosystem is important for several reasons including:

1. Open for freedom of speech, but protected for children and youth
2. Effective for government, but policed of abuse of power, political terrorism
3. Medically, physiologically, emotionally healthy for individuals and society
4. Productive for business, but safe from identity theft, financial crime
5. Freely, equally accessible to all users:

   a. Social digital divide
   b. Access digital divide
   c. Disabled, Section 508 users

6. Environmentally safe and conservative
7. Education: Omnipresent, open teaching, learning, research
8. Creative, innovative heights, human progress

It is important for all of us to start to see the bigger picture here in order to take the right steps all along the way when we are creating and maintaining our own Web content in any format. Often times it is not so obvious to see that the seemingly smaller decisions we make today can affect the larger context down the road.

4.1 Individual, Medium, Society

What we are effectively doing here is engineering the interface between the front end of the networked computer and us, the human users. It is important to keep this in mind and remember that information is around us all of the time. We could even say that information is *in* us. It's in us because we think about the information we have about the world around us all of the time. Think about when we are processing information about a place we are going or a person that we are meeting. Perhaps we already had some of this information prior to getting to this place or meeting this person. Some of us use maps to get directions before leaving the house all of the time. We perform Internet searches about people we are going to meet in order to find out a bit about them so that we are prepared.

We might even take this a step further and say that we are made of information. Without getting into a religious discussion, we know that the human reproductive

Fig. 4.1 Individual, information, and society. Information is signified here by the television, but this representation could just as easily be illustrated as the PC, laptop, or mobile device. It is important to note that it represents the role of information and how it is situated between the individual and the world around us

process passes on information coded in the form of DNA. We know we can inherit characteristics from our relatives. The fact that you have dark hair or light hair is not all by chance, the DNA, the coded information that your parents passed on to you plays a vital role.

Later in this book we look at how some philosophers of technology have investigated how information can actually change the ways in which we behave. The mass media, the news, advertisements, commercials, even the content of our personal media channels play a large role in how we perceive ourselves and others. All of these technologies may appear differently in our daily lives, and perhaps we interact with them to varying degrees and in different ways, however, the basic and common denominator here is information. All of these technologies disseminate information to us. We consume some of that information regularly. How much we consume and what we consume is up to us, the individual user (Fig. 4.1).

Chapter 5
The Real Discovery: The Web is Glial

Imagine yourself as a structural engineer. You've been fascinated with bridges of all kinds, styles, and sizes since you were a child. You built them with blocks, sticks, Erector sets, paper, and mashed potatoes on a regular basis until high school. In high school you joined the Bridge Builders Club and won blue ribbons with a team of other young structural enthusiasts your age for four years in a row. You easily made it into the top of your class at Old Cotcliff University[1] and studied, of course, bridge engineering. Now you have graduated from college and have a job in an outstanding firm. This is the ideal job for you. And now, you've just been commissioned to build the brand new Twostockshotstoke Bridge for the wonderful city of Lake Soletownersly. As you know, when a bridge needs to be built, it is a massive project in just about every way. It is up to you and your crack team of structural engineers to successfully and safely fulfill this bridge project. Everything that it takes to turn the empty space over Lake Soletownersly (the town is named after the enormous lake) is up to you, your abilities, and your experience in this field with this type of assignment.

After a few weeks of preliminary research you learn that Lake Soletownersly is the second highest alpine lake in the U.S. and the third largest alpine lake in the world. Commonly referred to as "The Sole," or just "Sole" by locals, beautiful blue Lake Soletownersly is located between the great regions of Browngroveside and Pitby Abbot in the North. Lake Soletownersly has a surface elevation of 6,229 ft., is 22 miles long, 12 miles wide and has a shoreline 71 miles in length. With a surface area of 193 square miles, a maximum depth of over 1,600 feet and an average depth of 989 feet, the total capacity of Lake Soletownersly is 122,160,280 acre-ft. (39 trillion gallons) of water. Surface lake temperatures range from 68 °F in the summer, to 41 °F during the winter. The only outlet is the Kiplockbrook River at Whenbank Hill. This is a big job and you have only just begun to gather preliminary information. How did you come to know this data?

---

[1] These place, town, lake names are fictional. They were generated with software "RaToNaGe." Random Town Name Generator (2011): n.pag. Web. 22 Dec 2012. http://www.mf2fm.com/RaToNaGe/

G. O'Toole, *Sustainable Web Ecosystem Design*,
SpringerBriefs in Computer Science, DOI: 10.1007/978-1-4614-7714-3_5,
© The Author(s) 2013

Certainly your firm could do the original measurements to learn this data. Perhaps, though, through local and national resources and databases the company acquired accurate, but already existing data.

Onward, you have many questions yet which need to be answered. Your team needs not only to manage to raise and connect the materials spanning the waters of Lake Soletownersly, but you have to tackle countless other aspects of a bridge construction project as well. Things like choosing the right type of bridge to build under these conditions, materials logistics, personnel management, payroll, crew scheduling, and many other variables. Where do you start? Well, you know that this type of bridge project has happened before. There are exactly twelve other bridges in the world that span an area the size of Lake Soletownersly. Many of these other bridges are sound, beautiful, and sustainable constructs. In other words, they were successful projects that output a successful product. This experience is a valuable asset to you and your team for the successful completion of Twostock-shotstoke Bridge. Those engineering equations, development logs, payroll procedures, construction blueprints, and logistics plans are all helpful in understanding those projects, and, therefore, they are helpful in understanding your project. Of course, you are not planning to copy those other bridges, you aspire to a revelation in innovative, unique beauty for your new project, but in many ways, you are going to recreate those other projects. You are going to replicate the science. There is a level of necessary human interaction and mediated communication that takes place in order for this transference of data. This information is saved by the engineering company and by the regulating municipalities that confirm that the projects are moving forward safely and according to proper building codes. In other words, most, if not all, of this bridge building project is information. This includes the bridges built in the past, and those that will come in the future.

The same scenario is true if you are running chemistry experiments in a lab, starting up a business, learning medicine, or studying techniques in snowman building. The commonality here is that sharing past experience is a key to human success. What did your mom do when she needed an old family baked bean or coconut cream pie recipe? She probably called a relative and wrote it down, right? How did you learn how to tie your shoes, twirl a baton, or catch a trout? You learned these basic skills from instruction, watching other people, being told the little secrets that bridge the time and space between failure and success. This is information. Good, useful, positive information is a bridge, not filler. The string loop techniques that an older sibling passes on to a younger brother or sister in order to tie a bow in a shoelace is pure information. The skills involved in how a baton spins in the palm of a child's hand, around their fingers, or through the air is pure information. Along with maybe a bit of luck, the full creel of Brookies on a spring day, as well as all of the ways those fish got into that wicker basket, is pure information.

Those construction and development logs from those twelve other bridges go into company files, local libraries or municipality offices. It's all information. The approvals, processes and results of the chemistry lab experiments go into academic or a scientific journal as data, reports, results: all information. These are the communiqués needed to do the science, to replicate the procedures toward some predictable end. It is all information and you can have access to it.

This transmission of information has always been magnificently important to human progress. Everything is based in information, and every step in our progress is a transmission of information. The Web has simply given us a rather user-friendly, easy, omnipresent interface to this all-important information. Now and going forward *this* is the role of the Web, the interface to information. The Web is both mechanism and metaphor for the informational space between your central nervous system and everyone you know and everyone you interact with personally, professionally, or otherwise.

The information is nearly all that matters in each of these examples. The Web is *used as* the planner, financial mechanism, project manager, social conduit, and communiqué for replicating proper behavior toward a successful result and therefore the Web *becomes* these things. This is another reason why the Web must be treated and maintained as a contemplative ecosystem. We must be conscientious of how we manage it because it plays this all-important role.

Until rather recently certain cells in the human brain were considered relatively unimportant to the primary functions of the central nervous system. In 1846 near what is now Berlin, Germany cellular pathologist Rudolf Virchow discovered Glia cells during his search for a connective tissue in the brain (Baumann, and Pham-Dinh 871–927). The term "glial" translates from the Greek as "glue" and is defined as "supportive, non-neuronal tissue of the nervous system" (OED Online). Early on in the time since Virchow's discovery the scientific community "assumed that glial cells were just structural filler" (Yuhas, and Jabr) at best, or didn't exist at all, at the very least. However, "these cells have come a long way within (the past) 20 years, from their existence being questioned (Dolman) to providing a potentially very elegant handle on the treatment of higher brain-functional defects (Chenet)" (Graeber 783–788). The neuroscience community has learned that these glia serve as the neurons' "helpmate: housekeeper, insulator, occasional nurse" supporting the processes of the neurons' themselves. We are starting to accept that the brain's "other half boasts a repertoire of functions every bit as vital as those of neurons" (Yuhas, and Jabr).

Today we know that it is the role of the glial cells to surround neurons and hold them in place, to supply nutrients and oxygen to neurons, to insulate one neuron from another, and to destroy pathogens and remove dead neurons.[2] Further, glial cells have been observed to communicate with one another as well as with neurons. Glia do not communicate electrically as is the case between neurons, but they communicate chemically. This is significant in that glia make up 85 % of the cells in the brain. At the same time, it is part of the reason scientists did not discover the full role of the glial cells until much later (Field).

---

[2] It is largely the general neuroscientific consensus that these are the known functions of glial cells. This list derived from Wikipedia: http://en.wikipedia.org/wiki/Neuroglia, on December 22, 2012.

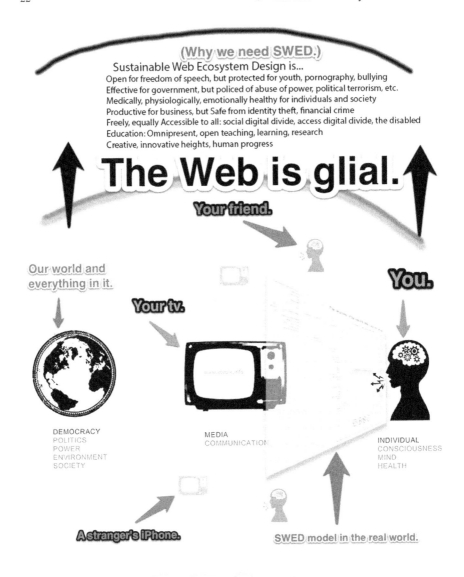

The Web is glial.

(Why we need SWED.)
Sustainable Web Ecosystem Design is...
Open for freedom of speech, but protected for youth, pornography, bullying
Effective for government, but policed of abuse of power, political terrorism, etc.
Medically, physiologically, emotionally healthy for individuals and society
Productive for business, but Safe from identity theft, financial crime
Freely, equally Accessible to all: social digital divide, access digital divide, the disabled
Education: Omnipresent, open teaching, learning, research
Creative, innovative heights, human progress

Your friend.

Our world and everything in it.

Your tv.

You.

DEMOCRACY
POLITICS
POWER
ENVIRONMENT
SOCIETY

MEDIA
COMMUNICATION

INDIVIDUAL
CONSCIOUSNESS
MIND
HEALTH

A stranger's iPhone.   SWED model in the real world.

Fig. 5.1 Context around the Web ecosystem. The anatomy of the sustainable Web ecosystem is shown here illustrating how it resides as an atmospheric environment between the brain of the individual user and society. In this context, society is simply a group of other individual users. The updated version of this infographic is freely available at http://www.otoole.info

Metaphorically speaking this *awareness* of the increased importance of these glial cells in the complex condition that is the human brain can be equated to the Web, for the Web is simply the interface to and the manifestation of information, that is, the important stuff that we need, use, and rely on every day and in every way. These glia, as far as we can tell, have always been a key element in the proper functioning of the central nervous system, that is, they have always been present and have always played a necessary role in life. It took time for the scientific community to learn that they exist, and it took more time to recognize and understand a fuller view of their necessity.

We seem to be in a similar state when it comes to the Web. As has been said, the Web is the interface to virtually unlimited amounts of information. As we know, information has always been a key element in the functioning of life, and not just human life, but all life. We are starting, in larger scale, to understand and except this now during the time of the advent of information technology and the Internet for mass, prolific use in our everyday. It is with this set of similarities and parallels in mind that, on the connected side of the access digital divide, that information accessible, editable, and transferrable through the Web acts as the glia property in contemporary life and has been positioned evolutionarily as a core necessity to just about everything we do, much like the function of the glial cells around the neurons in the brain. Therefore, we can say that neuroglia is to information as the *true* (or at least increased) *understanding* of neuroglia is to the Web (Fig. 5.1).

Chapter 6
Web User Research

Relating to the anatomy of sustainable Web ecosystem design there are different types of research that are worthwhile to discuss and this list is not in any way exhaustive. Some of these types of research are more traditional, and some are not. To be a Web designer, and most certainly a Web developer, one must be doing research as part of the daily practice. This is the case even though we may not look at it as work being done in a traditional research role. Rarely to design-developers or user interface engineers do the same things repeatedly day in and day out. Certainly there are recurring tasks, but the exploratory element to designing and developing new digital media and Web products is one based in research, and, of course, development. Design-developers need to be constantly aware of standards, protocols, syntax, and other best practices. Troubleshooting, code debugging, and other maintenance are all a big part of the design-developer's professional life. Often times documentation repositories and other discussion forums are used to create communities around, for example, open source software to share ideas, solutions, and to move the product and the community forward. This is a type of research.

At the same time, forward thinking in the field reveals a need for research into unknown and uncharted areas of information technology in many ways. One obvious ways of expressing this is the fact that there are entire colleges at research universities dedicated to the study of information, information sciences, and technology that are growing up all over the world. One of these areas is brain computer interface technology.

No matter what type of research you are involved with, interested in, or curious about, it is a necessary node that must be considered when mapping the anatomy of sustainable Web ecosystem design.

G. O'Toole, *Sustainable Web Ecosystem Design*,
SpringerBriefs in Computer Science, DOI: 10.1007/978-1-4614-7714-3_6,
© The Author(s) 2013

6.1 HCI/BCI

We have arrived at a point where we now need to specify our discourse about "HCI" or human-computer interface, and include the more direct process of "BCI" or brain-computer interface. Research toward the goal of understanding how we as users interact with our screens and the response the brain has to these interactions is a necessary node that must be considered when mapping the anatomy of sustainable Web ecosystem design.

Friedrich Kittler's exploration of media discourse analysis is greatly motivated with the theory that there needs to be a necessary pursuit toward the development of the *science of media* (Medienwissenschaft), pressing at the intrinsic obligations of a hard science, to arrive at the potential of investigative efforts into its own inherent natures and behaviors. Kittler holds that if this call-to-duty is not attained by contemporary scholars of media in a way more directly involved than cultural practitioners who "know higher mathematics only from hearsay," (Kittler 219) what will be carried out, essentially, is nothing more than an exaggeration continuum of the mere history of media.

In my agreement with Kittler, my response to this is to evolve a project and work as the principal researcher and test coordinator with a small group of academic, technical, and research professionals in the U.S. and Canada on studying the neurophysiological effects of media use and human cognition. To date, the research is being done using electroencephalography (EEG) to examine brain wave activity in subjects during their use of various digital screen and analog codex media. Preliminary testing has been done across a multitude of media technologies. Currently the project is in search of long-term funding opportunities.

This research project is aimed at scientifically determining the differences in human brain experience when reading "traditional," (paper) codex book versus the same content on screen, on both mobile, native format devices, and larger screen Web-based media. The tests will look for and document any change (or lack thereof) in the brainwave activity of the occipital and parietal lobes specifically.

This study, initially suggested via the MEA by Eric McLuhan, was to be based on Herbert Krugman's earlier tests of a similar nature. In 1969, Krugman researched the brain waves in the occipital lobe of a subject via EEG and compared the neuroactivity during the activities of watching television advertisements and various print media magazine advertisements. McLuhan suggested that a series of similar EEG comparisons be run with varied subjects in varied locations to compare the brain wave patterns of a subject reading from a traditional, paper (codex) book and an e-ink device such as the currently popular Amazon Kindle[TM].

Our hypothesis in this study was only to test for and document any change (or lack thereof) in the brain wave activity of the occipital and parietal lobes of the subject while reading a codex book compared to reading a version of the same content on an e-ink device.

For this set of tests the subject was connected to a Nihon Kohden[TM] brand Electroencephalographic machine. The computer was a Dell[TM] Optiplex[TM]

GX260 running Windows 2000 Professional (NT)^{TM} operating system. The software used was Neurofax^{TM} v04-03. The test was administered by a registered EEG technician of 30+ years of professional service in the neurology lab of a leading hospital in the United States. The longitudinal bipolar montage (double banana) was used. The montage constituting these examinations was made up of 19 channels of data originating from 22 electrodes utilizing a differential amplifier. One channel was the EKG (electrocardiogram) detection. The following activating procedures were measured over a 10-min time period for each. The subject: at rest with eyes closed, at rest with eyes open, reading a paperback codex book, reading an e-ink device with identical content as the book. The textual content was the chapter titled "The Sisters" from James Joyce's *Dubliners*.

After the tests were run the channel data from four channels was examined. The four channels examined were P3-O1, P4-O2, T5-O1, and T6-O2. These four channels were chosen because they reflect the activity in the occipital lobe (visual cortex, visual processing) and parietal lobe (spatial navigation, sensory information) of the brain.

A brief time period was examined for each of these four channels in the EEG results. (Further tests will be done to include longer time frames for further proof in accuracy.) Within each of these time periods, the channel data (EEG waves) were broken down into 1-s time frames each. The waves in each 1-s time frame were counted and placed into the following brain wave categories, as are the standardized brain wave categories.

It is important to note here that this test is being based off of previous EEG and media use tests including Krugman, Radlick, etc. The chart in Table 6.1 describing each brain wave range is the same as is used in these tests. There are other materials and references available that use a slightly different chart. For example, Krugman's studies describe the Alpha range from 8 to 12 Hz. Other materials describe the Alpha range from 8 to 13 Hz (see Table 6.1).

The total number of seconds for each range was totaled up. This figure was then calculated as a percentage of the total time period in order to know how much of the total time period showed beta waves, how much of the total time period showed alpha waves, etc.

The chart in Table 6.1 illustrates the type, the frequency range, the location (when available), the amplitude (when available), and the behavioral associations of each of the wave pattern categories tested for in the research project.

The results of this study focused only on the occipital and parietal related channels of data from the EEG tests recording the test subject at rest with eyes closed, reading a book, and reading an e-ink device. (Due to a differing number of seconds counted in the book test than in the e-ink and resting tests, the emphasis is put on the percentage of the total time that was each type, not the total number of seconds. This will be corrected for in future tests.)

The chart shown in Table 6.2 illustrates the results based on data calculation.

It is concluded from this experiment that, although the numbers shift slightly within the beta range (from beta to high beta, or beta to low beta), that there is only

Table 6.1 The brain wave pattern recognition chart used in these examinations

Type/Range	Frequency (Hz)	Location	Amplitude	Association
Gamma	25/30–100	–	–	Thought to represent binding of different populations of neurons together
Hi-Beta	19–25	–	–	Active periods Motor activity Concentration Decision Making
Beta	15–18	–	<25 µV, at times can be higher	Active periods Motor activity Concentration Decision Making
Low-Beta	12 (14[a])–15	–	–	Active periods Motor activity Concentration Decision Making
Alpha	8–12 (13[b])	Occipital–parietal region	10–150 µV	Relaxed Posterior basic rhythm
Theta	4–7	Variable	Variable	Memory Daydream Meditation
Delta	Up to 3	Variable	Variable	Rest Sleep Dreaming

It is important to note the differences in assumed frequency ranges from the different sources, particularly in the low beta and alpha ranges
[a] A textbook that has been used for many years (EEG Handbook, 2nd Edition. Craib, Alice, Perry, Margaret. Beckman, 1975) to train electroencephalographic technicians and radiologists has the low beta range spanning from 14–15 Hz
[b] A textbook that has been used for many years (EEG Handbook, 2nd Edition. Craib, Alice, Perry, Margaret. Beckman, 1975) to train electroencephalographic technicians and radiologists has the alpha range spanning from 8–13 Hz

this slight variation in the neuroactivity of the occipital and parietal lobes when reading a codex book compared to reading e-ink technology.

However, it has been realized through this preliminary examination that there is certainly a need for further research in this area. In further testing we tried also to "read" a Web page containing the *Dubliners* text which also contained links, navigation, advertisement images and text, video, headlines, suggested links and other Web content. This condition showed a very different EEG. This condition produced a majority of high beta waves. One possible reason for this heighted set of brain waves is that beta waves characterize decision-making and a higher concentration mode of cognition (than alpha) among other characteristics. This portion of the experiment most closely fit with Krugman's findings.

Further, on a second day of testing, more conditions were included. These conditions were video/TV watching, listening only to audio, looking at still images, and browsing/reading a magazine. But if Krugman's results are valid, and Alpha was found during TV and beta during magazine, it could be that there are "no real decisions" being made while watching TV and therefore the more relaxed alpha state. Meanwhile, during magazine experience, shorter text blocks, images, sidebars, captions, etc. there are many more decisions and quick cognitions going on, much like a slightly less dynamic, and finite type of Web experience. It is possible that in comparison to the much older, more simplified 1969 television set, today's televisions with multi-feature remotes, window in window and other multi-optional views, news and sports tickers, animated in screen ads, Web interaction, and other interactivities, may start to produce more beta during our television consumption as well.

Suggested Web Resource(s):

Web Use Brain Response Research: http://www.otoole.info.
Penn State Media Effects Research Lab: http://www.psu.edu/dept/medialab.
Penn State Social, Life, Engineering Imaging Center: http://www.imaging.psu.edu.

Table 6.2 BCI research results

Type	Book		e-ink		Rest	
	No.	%	No.	%	No.	%
Gamma	0	0	0	0	0	0
Hi-beta	6	21.4	11	34	0	0
Beta	21	75	19	59	0	0
Low-beta	1	3.5	2	6.25	0	0
Alpha	0	0	0	0	32	100
Theta	0	0	0	0	0	0
Delta	0	0	0	0	0	0

The results of the experiment based on the data calculations are shown here

6.2 Surveys

Surveying or "benchmarking" what is currently online is a key step in gauging existing ideas that are already in production. Don't think of this as cheating or stealing from, for example, another Web site if you are working on creating a new Web site of your own. Think of this as a type of literature review step in your preparation and research toward your new project. It is important to know what is out there, what is being done, how things are being done, and where the "cutting edge" resides so that you can orient your project relevant to this edge.

6.3 Usability

Usability is about as ambiguous a topic as you can find. However, generally it is accurate when we talk about usability of a Web ecosystem in terms how easy or difficult, fun or boring, cool or lame, fast or slow, exciting or tedious the actual human interaction is with the Web site, mobile app, game, or other interactive environment that we are using. It can be just that simple. Of course, as designers, developers, stakeholders, and users of an interactive system, for the most part, we prefer it if the responsiveness of the technology we are using is somehow positive. Nobody wants to deal with a difficult, confusing, slow application whether they are doing a task at work, playing a game for entertainment, or checking sports scores. We want our experiences to be interesting.

To help in the process of making more interesting systems we can do usability testing on the interfaces and interactivity we are building. There are many ways in which you can do usability testing from very casual, 2-min tests to long-term, involved experiments. Usability is a necessary node that must be considered when mapping the anatomy of sustainable Web ecosystem design.

Some of what we can test for in Web usability experiments:

- How user interacts with screen
- Do they use search or navigate
- Do they use mobile
- Can they access all info
- Pleased or frustrated
- Duration of stay
- Frequency of visit
- Where to users go
- What do they do
- Eye tracking
- Neuroresponse

6.4 Focus Groups

A quick query for "Web focus groups" on Google Scholar displays nearly three million results. Of course, not all of these are highly relevant, but it does illustrate the wide acceptance, use, and attention paid to focus groups. Focus groups can be highly useful in designing for specific, target audiences. A useful focus group for your project is a selection of potential users. Choose a small sample from your target user base and begin to formulate questions that will give you insight into how they use your project, what their experiences are, and how they like it or dislike it. Focus groups work much like usability testing for a group. Depending on your project and the target audience you have established, focus groups may be a very useful resource in understanding your target demographic, what they expect from your project, how they interact with it, and what their skill levels are. Each of these variables allows you to fine-tune your project to suit their background and abilities, all with the goal of making the project's user experience as seamless as possible.

6.5 Web User Profiles

Knowing your audience is very important when you're designing Web sites. Many designers do not take a critical look at whom they are developing for and often fall short because of it. To this end, we will begin to look at a process known as an audience analysis. This process will form a foundation for many of the Web-based projects a designer will undertake.

This topic is designed for you to gather information about usability, accessibility, and information architecture as it relates to the World Wide Web. We will tackle issues associated with using the results of the audience analysis to build the appropriate levels of navigation and end user aides to allow people to use your site as it is intended.

At a rapid rate, much of the world is coming online, and individuals are connecting with each other regardless of the physical distance that separates them. Many bridges are being built to circumvent centralized authority, join individuals of common interests, and create new communities.

Creating a successful Web site involves much more than just creating and implementing a few Web pages. Careful consideration needs to be given to the intended end user, or audience, of your site. Be sure to pay attention to limitations your intended end user may have. The last thing a developer wants to do is create a site that several people cannot view due to their physical or technological limitations.

When designing information for the World Wide Web, one of the primary areas a designer should focus on is the needs and capabilities of the end users. Without gaining a complete and detailed understanding of the end users of the site, a lot of time and money may be spent designing and developing a site that is not functional, thus useless to end users.

One way of gathering end user information is audience analysis, or end user analysis. The purpose of an audience analysis is to identify any and all limitations and capabilities that the end users may have (which may prevent them from viewing the site).

Audience Analysis can be very insightful for your project. Specifically, an audience analysis is used to answer questions such as:

- What type of computer system/operating system will the end users have?
- What type of Internet connection do the end users have?
- What language do they speak?
- With what browser(s) and version(s) of the browser(s) do the end users view Web sites?
- What software or plug-ins do the end users have or use?
- What are the computer system settings of the end users?
- Is your audience media literate?
- What is their technical competency?

By understanding the end users' capabilities, designers and developers can focus on implementing technologies that can be viewed by each of the users. When making site design decisions, it is good practice to develop the site utilizing only those technologies that will allow the user with the lowest common capability to view the site. If you cannot gather this end user data, go with the lowest common current standards. For example, if the audience analysis shows that a majority of the users of the site use Firefox 2.0, then the site should include only those technologies that can be viewed in Firefox 2.0 or higher.

Currently there is work being done to qualitatively and quantitatively map a set of universal Web user profiles.[1] Accurately understanding your user profiles is a necessary node that must be considered when mapping the anatomy of sustainable Web ecosystem design.

Suggested Web Resource(s):

Web User Profile Research: http://www.otoole.info.

---

[1] This research is currently being done within the College of Information Sciences and Technology at The Pennsylvania State University at University Park, PA. Principle Investigator Gregory O'Toole.

Chapter 7
The Project

Although there are any number of effective points of entry to a Web system project, many times we start with a concept, a need, and/or a story that moves the project forward from the point of being "just an idea." Where an idea or need comes from is usually not something we need to spend much time on simply because in today's busy world there is often times no shortage of them. Artists and entrepreneurs deal on the cutting edge of innovative ideas, and that is not out of the scope of the ideas of this book so it is certainly worth a good amount of thought. Without getting too philosophical here on the origins of ideas in the minds and brains of their thinkers,[1] we can start to talk about some key elements of your project concepts such as vision, brand or message, communication and a balanced media ecosystem. Therefore it is without uncertainty that concept is a necessary node that must be considered when mapping the anatomy of sustainable Web ecosystem design.

7.1 Vision

Dream big. The sky is the limit on what you can do with today's media communication technologies. Know your timeline if you have one. Don't take on too much at once. Work incrementally. Make progress. The vision of a project may be ideological in nature, but it gives substance to and ideal goal. The vision is what you share with your team, consultants, clients, stakeholders, anyone involved in the grand production of what it is you are working toward. How to arrive at a

---

[1] There have been works written that address the issue of the origin of ideas and concepts. One suggestion is: O'Toole, Gregory. "The Machined Word." The International Journal of the Arts in Society, Vol 2, No. 3. ISSN 1833-1866. Common Ground Publishing. 2007. For another start to this open-ended question, see "The Powers and Perils of Intuition" in Psychology Today by David G. Myers, published on November 01, 2002, last retrieved 23 Dec 2012 from http://www.psychologytoday.com/articles/200212/the-powers-and-perils-intuition. Malcom Gladwell's Blink: The Power of Thinking Without Thinking (Back Bay Books; 1 edition, April 3, 2007) is an interesting survey of intuitive "thin slicing" across history.

G. O'Toole, *Sustainable Web Ecosystem Design*,
SpringerBriefs in Computer Science, DOI: 10.1007/978-1-4614-7714-3_7,
© The Author(s) 2013

common vision is beyond the scope of this book, however the need or story that was discussed in the previous section is often times the catalyst for any project. To get things off the ground brainstorming and idea mapping can really start to move things along. However the need for your project arises, a common vision is necessary for your entire team. This makes vision is a necessary node that must be considered when mapping the anatomy of sustainable Web ecosystem design.

7.2 Brand/Message

Your brand is your one-word, first impression on the world. Brand recognition is a topic that is heavily covered in both academic programs as well as in industry. It is a multi-trillion dollar a year industry around the world. With the early use of crude black and white images in magazines and newspapers in the later nineteenth century we began to see the image emerging as the powerhouse in communication we know it to be today. A movement in advertising-based identity and brand recognition erupted in the 1920s in New York City. The popular metonym, of course, is Madison Avenue. The seemingly unlimited power of image recognition to sell products and services was born. What was once thought of as a memorable jingle, tag line, logo, or slogan has been distilled down to a science in its own right, quite literally. The effective communication of your brand is a necessary node that must be considered when mapping the anatomy of sustainable Web ecosystem design.

7.3 Communication

It is necessary in a dialog to have an open consensus on the communication framework of the discussion. Before a discussion can properly begin to take place the framework around which the conversation is going to take place must be agreed upon by all parties (i.e. both sides) of a discussion. This includes vocabulary, political points of view, subjects, topics, characters involved and their historical backgrounds. Clarifying these elements of a conversation is necessary to level the playing field, and create the conditions that are most conducive to an open and clear discussion. To skip this step leaves hidden too many factors that can become blockades or points of distraction, or worse, departure from the initial topic. Defining vocabulary words, for example, is usually reserved for academic analyses. We don't usually start a conversation with an acquaintance on a controversial soccer match played the night before by explaining what we mean when we say Didier Drogba is a top player and therefore Chelsea should not have allowed him to leave the club because we assume each participant in the conversation understands what it means to be a top player. As you start to break down, though, what it means to you for a player to be considered "top," are these the same necessary attributes that others in the conversation retain on their list of criteria? Sometimes they may be the same as those on your list, but not always. Different people will have different constitutions for what needs to be considered in order for a player to be considered one of the best. The different lists, in fact, may be completely different all together. What of the list of requirements for a player to be a top forward, a top goal scorer, a top defender, a top goalie, a top captain, etc. This is the necessity of this step in the post-legitimation model. These variables need to be established, and be clarified early on and in a way that each individual in the conversation is in agreement. It is not required that this be a universal agreement, that what is agreed on for a player to be a top forward be agreed on for this conversation and every conversation that individual has from then on. This is not necessary. What is necessary is that the terms and other variables in a conversation be clarified and agreed on by all participants in this conversation. If this agreement can be carried forward to future conversations, so be it, this is an added benefit to the current condition. Communication is a necessary node that must be considered when mapping the anatomy of sustainable Web ecosystem design.

7.4 Balanced Media Ecosystem

Media Ecology is a field of study that focuses on many ideas pertaining to media studies. One founding idea proposed years ago by Marshal McLuhan is the idea of maintaining a balanced media environment so that one media type does not cancel out other media types. This idea of balance and leverage, to create as efficient a system as possible, is an important one to keep in mind as you work to create a sustainable web ecosystem of your own which will plug into a greater informational Web system. A balanced media ecosystem is a necessary element in the anatomy of sustainable Web ecosystem design.

Suggested Web Resource(s):

Media Ecology on Wikipedia: http://en.wikipedia.org/wiki/Media_ecology.

Chapter 8
Project Management

Leadership is important. Be the leader. Look around, the world has been completely constructed by people who are often times no smarter than you. Project management is a necessary node that must be considered when mapping the anatomy of sustainable Web ecosystem design.

8.1 Pre-production

Pre-production is the time and place where most of your preliminary planning occurs. These may seem like small steps at first, but they are rather inclusive and certainly are a necessary part of the anatomy of sustainable Web ecosystem design.

8.1.1 Concept Document/Functional Specification

Creating effective projects usually requires multiple people. Having a clear blueprint is key to starting off on common ground, with everyone involved knowing they are on the same page as the rest of the team. Planning is a necessary node that must be considered when mapping the anatomy of sustainable Web ecosystem design. Ideally, what you want to come away with after a successful planning and research (i.e. pre-production) stage is one clear, competent document (any format) that you can hand off to another designer, developer, engineer, programmer, project manager, client, colleague, or stake holder and be confident that they will be able to get up to speed quickly and understand, if not accurately visualize, your project plans. Your concept document should be clear and concise. More importantly, it should be accurate. Don't guess at the components—find out exactly where you stand. You will build your project from this document. You certainly don't want to be halfway through development and realize that one of your initial statements is not accurate. Save yourself needless headaches and

G. O'Toole, *Sustainable Web Ecosystem Design*,
SpringerBriefs in Computer Science, DOI: 10.1007/978-1-4614-7714-3_8,
© The Author(s) 2013

potential disasters by being well prepared upfront. This planning is a necessary part of the anatomy of sustainable Web ecosystem design. Other suggested key nodes in this development plan which can be addressed early on in the planning of a project are:

Clear Objectives—After you have dreamed big and created visionary ideals. Scale it down, make it realistic and set clear objectives. Clarity around the objectives of a project is a necessary node that must be considered when mapping the anatomy of sustainable Web ecosystem design.

Goals—Setting clear goals is a necessary part of the anatomy of sustainable Web ecosystem design. A product plan needs to identify clear milestones in development called goals. A goal is a measurable, tangible outcome. It is a point where you have significant product advancement no matter how large or small the step may be. Goals are stated factually, and are best stated clearly and concisely, not in a way that is difficult to define. Vaguely documented goals do not provide the team with the specifics of time and place that are necessary to maintain clear communication. Terms like "ongoing" and "develop this first" do not clearly define what is being done and when it must be completed.

Goals may be somewhat of a judgment call, especially early in the project life span. There is no universal set of standards for what goals should be included in your plan because they will differ for your unique project. A good project manager looks for the milestones that should occur over the development cycle and typically states them as his or her goals. The first time you set out to create a set of goals for a project, you will inevitably feel a bit overwhelmed. It is natural to do one of two things: assess too many goals (which leaves you with no real gauge to stop and observe the development) or underestimate major milestones (leaving your development cycle with major holes that could potentially cause problems in the delivery of the final project). Creating realistic goals is a learned skill—one that is the result of accumulated experience. You're bound to make some mistakes. You will also do something very right that you didn't even plan on. As you create more and more product plans, you will put those learned lessons to use. The best advice in planning that a novice can take is to approach the plan calmly, trying to picture each step, from day one to the final day of the project. After you do that, look at what you have listed, go back and ask yourself, "Where are the milestones?" Remember, milestones are logical points of accomplishment, points at which a significant portion of your daily work culminates to create the next level of the product's development.

Once you have established your goals for the development of the product, it's time to get to the details of the production planning process—defining the specific actions that support the goals and assigning accountability. Action plans, like goals, are statements of fact. Terms like "It would be nice to have" or "hopefully we will" have no place in your action plans. Action plans are all business. Remember, action plans support goals. Once you have a set of goals, you should review each and assign the most complete list of action plans that you can imagine are necessary to successfully support the goal.[1]

Potential Need—Clearly establish the potential need for you product. Simply asking the question "Why am I making this?" can address this part of your project. This is a necessary part of the anatomy of sustainable Web ecosystem design.

Genre/Theme—Genre or theme goes hand in hand with the branding and identity of your project. These plans should be included in this documentation.

Technology Requirements—Technology requirements and abilities of your target user base are established in the research part of your project. They should be included in this documentation.

Product Introduction—A product introduction is a clearly written explanation of your project. You will find that during the lifespan of a project you will have uses for versions of this introduction of different lengths. It is recommended to write a short, medium, and long version of a product introduction.

1. Short—The summative 5 sentences you can pull from this for use in certain situations where quickness and brevity pays.
2. Medium—About 1/3 to 1/2 of the amount you have here. Useful as, maybe, the "About" or "Home" page of a web site.
3. Long—Everything you have here. Think of the uses for the short or medium versions to have a "Read more..." link.

Preliminary Product Designs—Preliminary product designs are important in order to communicate your ideas and progress to the team and stakeholders.

Product Components/Flowchart/Wireframes—Use the site's visual design to establish a hierarchy of content. Many sites seem cluttered and confusing because the site designer failed to identify what was most important, and thus made too many links visible on any one page. You (possibly in consultation with your client, whether internal or external) need to figure out what's important: make that big and make what's less important small. Once you determine the priorities, it will be much easier to figure out where the pieces are supposed to go. Flowcharting a Web site is very useful when developers are still in the design process. It is much cheaper to create a flowchart of the site, and make changes on the flowchart, than it is to start programming and make ongoing changes throughout the development of the site. Flowcharts can be used to graphically map out the flow of a Web site. Many developers have created their own unique symbols and numbering system when dealing with flowcharts. In most cases, each symbol on a flowchart

---

[1] Some good advice on setting and managing project goals was given in the course content for IMD411 Senior Research offered by the Department of Web Design and Interactive Media at The Art Institute of Pittsburgh Online Division.

represents a screen within a site. This stage in the planning is a necessary part of the anatomy of sustainable Web ecosystem design.

Product Diagrams/Storyboards—A well-developed storyboard also allows you to show your client what you have in mind before any actual coding begins. If you have a storyboard that both you and your client agree on, fewer "surprises" will occur during the development phase. With a well-developed storyboard, you can develop each page in turn without "missing" something, making testing and debugging a site that much easier.

You don't have to be able to draw to produce a storyboard. You need only sketch in the outlines. You can draw all this in simple shapes with a few notes. "This page is a white background, the navigation links go here and point to," and so on. The usual purpose of the storyboard is to communicate your prospective development intentions, not to win an art prize. However, if you are attempting to sell the idea of the Web site to a customer, you may want a storyboard that would win a prize.

Ideally, someone should be able to look at your storyboard, no matter how crude, and—using the right material—put together the same site you would have done. If you have a large site to develop, this can be very useful, allowing you to distribute work to others. From the storyboard they should be able to develop the pages as you want them. When you assemble the project, you should have consistently designed pages despite having several different authors. This is a necessary part of the anatomy of sustainable Web ecosystem design.

Market Factors—Researching and documenting current and potential future market factors can be invaluable to your project and the extent to which it succeeds.

Concept Document—The concept document is useful in collecting all of this documentation into one comprehensive document. Often times this documents is also referred to as a design spec. The functional specification document is an exhaustive compilation of what the product is all about, including:

- Product description
- Product designs
- The components of the product
- Specific diagrams of how the product works
- Market factors and user information
- Software and hardware requirements.

This document is the definitive source for what the product should be. It provides you with rules and guidelines for product creation. Successful delivery rests in you and your team's ability to follow your design spec to the letter.

You need to understand that your design spec is a complete picture of the product and how it works from the user's perspective—it is not a schedule, action plan, or implementation document. In fact, most good product managers will tell you that you cannot schedule and plan the production of a product until you have completed and finalized this document. Your design spec should answer all the questions someone building the product would have about how it works.[2]

8.1.2 Competitive Matrix

A competitive matrix is effective in analyzing the qualitative marketing viability of a product by gathering information about the competition. The competitive landscape section identifies who is out there in the marketplace and what they are doing. As your previous research in the competitive analysis and matrix indicated, you want to create a product that does certain things and serves certain people. Your product will exist as a choice amongst other relevant alternative products. Why would people choose your product? This section of your design spec shows the reader those features and benefits and explains how your product fits into the field.[3]

8.1.3 Cost Benefit Analysis

No designer ever likes to talk about the limitations imposed by costs. It is against a creative nature to limit your expression for an extra nickel or dime. But the reality is that cost to create is often the number one consideration of most products' development. The interactive designer who appreciates the cost-benefit relationship is a much wiser and effective advocate for his or her project.

There is no standard format for a cost-benefit analysis. Rather, it is a way of systematically justifying product features and discarding others based on the amount of money it will take to implement them. The documents that you have researched and created to this point will serve as the data for making your cost decisions. Your creative concept analysis will be the first step. It reminds you of the intent and purposes of the development. Your competitive analysis should provide you with an extensive list of features for the products and the relative benefit such features provide the user. You and your team might have to spend time reviewing each feature and placing a value on its importance. You might find

---

[2] Some good advice on organizing a concept document skeleton is given in the course content for IMD411 Senior Research offered by the Department of Web Design and Interactive Media at The Art Institute of Pittsburgh Online Division.

[3] Some good advice on establishing a competitive matrix is given in the course content for IMD411 Senior Research offered by the Department of Web Design and Interactive Media at The Art Institute of Pittsburgh Online Division.

features that offer little competitive advantage in relation to the costs they represent.

The important thing to remember about your cost-benefit analysis is that if your initial research has been clear, complete, and accurate, then this analysis will be fairly easy to complete. Like all producers of interactive products, one has to make some informed decisions about what can and can't be done in this round of development. This is a necessary part of the anatomy of sustainable Web ecosystem design.[4]

8.2 Team Roles and Methods

In any Web or software project there is some times opportunity, and often times direct necessity for working on a team that is made up of individuals with specializations in the different areas of Web technology and design.

Agile methodology is a faster way to design and develop and get the product you are creating into the hands of the people you are creating it for. Go from drawing board to iPad fast. Efficient team progress is a necessary node that must be considered when mapping the anatomy of sustainable Web ecosystem design.

8.2.1 Development Team Roles and Responsibilities

A Web Project Manager's responsibilities include:

- Assigning project tasks
- Running project meetings
- Setting the tone and course of a project
- Being capable of envisioning both logistical details and long-term results
- Familiarity with Web design technology and development in order to make appropriate decisions regarding a given project
- Delegating responsibilities and trusting team members to get the job done
- At times, being responsible for aspects of client relations, legal issues, and fiscal concerns
- Being diplomatic and understanding corporate and organizational politics.

Additional roles include experts from the following areas:

- Content providers/designers
- Interface designers (also named Human-Computer Interface (HCI) experts)

---

[4] Some good advice on calculating and documenting a cost benefit analysis is given in the course content for IMD411 Senior Research offered by the Department of Web Design and Interactive Media at The Art Institute of Pittsburgh Online Division.

- Graphic designers
- HTML developers
- Programmers (client and server side)
- Database administrators
- Systems administrators
- Marketing experts.

8.3 Source Code Management

Organization, backup, and version control are key to any large project. There are many solutions. Use them. Most good ones are free. Many good ones are anyway. Good source code management is a necessary part of the anatomy of sustainable Web ecosystem design.

Suggested Web Resource(s):

BitBucket: http://www.bitbucket.org
GitHub: http://www.github.org

8.4 Development Journal

A design or development journal is a companion along the way of creating your Web project. The details of this companion are completely up to you. What you are comfortable doing here is important. How you choose to layout the design journal is totally up to you. You can keep it in a word processing document, a notebook, a personal information manager—anything you are comfortable with. The important aspects of the design journal are:

The timeline of the process: You should clearly delineate the creative process so that when you refer to it in the future, you have a reasonable indication of how long each of the various processes will take you to complete.

The rationale for your decisions: Why did you choose to make the background a solid blue as opposed to a bitmap photo of space? What motivated you to use cartoon animations as opposed to video? Why did you produce the project in Flash rather than Director? You are accountable for your actions whenever you undertake a design project.

The design journal will help you remember the reasons you chose to do the things you did. This can be helpful when presenting products to your clients and also to keep you focused on the project at hand. There will always be a time, somewhere late in the project, when you may become frustrated with an element or operation and you will want to change it. Referring to the history of the item in your journal will help you to focus on your decision.

What went wrong and what went right: Believe it or not, the best use of this journal will be when you undertake a similar project in the future. If you honestly and objectively document the processes you followed, you ultimately learn from your triumphs and your mistakes. A design journal will help you to become a better designer over time.

Examples and supporting documents: Your design journal should be appended with everything that was part of the creative process. Save notes from meetings, roughs, supporting research, and reports—anything and everything that helped to guide you on the journey. You don't necessarily have to include the content of each of these various documents in the journal—keep copies of the files or the hard copies in a folder and reference them as needed.

The important point to remember about your design journal is that it is a personal log of your creative process. It is not a report for a client or facilitator to critique. It is not a document that needs to be perfectly written and free of mis-spellings. It is not for anyone else's use or reference except your own. It is your personal documentation of a creative and technical journey.

- Organize your thoughts, ideas, and action plans based on the process of your project including dates and other milestones
- Focus on the issues that revolved around decisions you have made throughout the process
- Explain actions you took during the creation process
- Document technical issues you encountered and what solutions worked and which ones did not, include code here as needed
- Produce more creative and technically accurate projects of this type in the future.[5]

---

[5] Some good advice on using development journals is given in the course content for IMD411 Senior Research offered by the Department of Web Design and Interactive Media at The Art Institute of Pittsburgh Online Division.

Chapter 9
Architecture

Information architecture is about planning the structure of a site so it is usable, accessible, and easy to maintain. It involves reflecting the attitude, feel, and tone of what the site is about. It involves systems of layout, labeling, navigation, and search to help people find and manage information more successfully. It also involves the physical layout of the page relationships. Good planning is crucial. Make sure both the originators' and the end-users' rights and privileges are served equally and well.

Attention to detail and a strong sense of organization are the most necessary skills for an information architect. The process of information architecture design begins with research into mission, vision, content, and audience. Well-designed information architecture minimizes the time that users of a Web site spend looking for information. A logical architecture is another necessary node that must be considered when mapping the anatomy of sustainable Web ecosystem design.

9.1 Web Content Management Systems

Although certainly not required to create and maintain a successful Web site, a Web Content Management Systems (CMS) can save a site developer a lot of work. CMS's allow for relatively quick setup and creation of the framework for a Web site and populate it with information via menus and checkboxes. Little, if any, actual HTML coding is required by the people that contribute content to the site. The administrator can easily control the look of the site via "skins," or graphical designs that are usually created with Cascading Style Sheets (CSS).

The administrator of the CMS can assign roles to individuals, giving them more or less power and capabilities as desired. Thus, some people may be able to add new content, while others can only comment on existing content. Because of the open nature of these CMS, where individuals can contribute to the site's content, they are considered a Web 2.0 technology. Some of the more commonly used CMS include WordPress, Drupal, Joomla, and Plone.

G. O'Toole, *Sustainable Web Ecosystem Design*,
SpringerBriefs in Computer Science, DOI: 10.1007/978-1-4614-7714-3_9,
© The Author(s) 2013

Suggested Web Resource(s):

Plone: http://www.plone.org
Drupal: http://www.drupal.org
Joomla: http://www.joomla.org
WordPress: http://www.wordpress.org
CMS on Wikipedia: http://en.wikipedia.org/wiki/Content_management_system
CMS on Open Directory Project: http://www.dmoz.org/Computers/Software/
Internet/Site_Management/Content_Management

9.2 Taxonomy

We are familiar with the idea and use of taxonomy by way of the life sciences, which use taxonomy as a way to hierarchically organize all life forms. Additionally, information and library sciences are fields that specialize in processes and methods of information search and retrieval. When we talk about and practice taxonomy in the Web context we are discussing the most effective ways in which we can organize Web-based content with the ultimate goal of making this information as accessible as possible, and in the easiest ways, for the largest base of our users. Like all parts of this book, taxonomy practices intersect with most all other areas of Web construction, including Web site design, content management, and Web search processes.

Mainly what we are concerned with here is presenting our Web content logically by grouping information into topics. We can do this by structure and/or by using tags, or keywords, to collect our Web content into sensible groups to "create a positive Web navigation experience through intuitive organization and labeling" (*TechRepublic*) that will ultimately be helpful to our users.

With increasing quantities of information on the Web we see the importance of taxonomy's critical role in Web structure and search by pointing out that "integrating taxonomy throughout the Web search process, we can provide a more efficient search experience. Less time is wasted in failed searches or in finding the wrong information, thereby facilitating an effective decision-making process" (*TechRepublic*). Taxonomy and logical, user-friendly vocabularies are necessary nodes that must be considered when mapping the anatomy of sustainable Web ecosystem design.

Suggested Web Resource(s):

TechRepublic Article: http://www.techrepublic.com/article/information-taxonomy-plays-a-critical-role-in-web-site-design-and-search-processes/5054221

9.3 Intuitive Tagging

Tagging content is the human-use side of taxonomy. If taxonomy is the hierarchical structure of categories to organize the information on a Web site, tagging is an intuitive way of putting content objects into these categories. The tagging of content with user-friendly and machine-friendly naming conventions is a necessary node that must be considered when mapping the anatomy of sustainable Web ecosystem design.

Suggested Web Resource(s):

Semantic Studios: http://semanticstudios.com

Suggested Book(s):

Ambient Findability by Peter Morville: http://shop.oreilly.com/product/978059 6007652.do

9.4 SEO Optimization

Making sure that potential users can find your project through Internet search engines is a necessary node that must be considered when mapping the anatomy of sustainable Web ecosystem design. We automatically setup your website to be well optimized for search engines through the use of sitemaps, automated pinging of new content, proper HTML formatting, and meta descriptions and keywords. More advanced search engine optimization settings are available as well, such as alt tags on images and page-specific descriptions, external links pointing to, and history duration.

Suggested Web Resource(s):

Google's SEO Guide: http://bit.ly/uRFyiL

Chapter 10
Functionality

Functionality is a necessary node that must be considered when mapping the anatomy of sustainable Web ecosystem design. Among other key elements in the area of functionality, it is important to have a basic understanding of the roles of protocols, hypertexts, and Web browsers, as these are the ways in which Web functionality is made technically possible.

There were two developments that are responsible for the Web, as we know it today: the development of the protocols for the Internet and the development of hypertext. The World Wide Web (WWW) is a set of Internet protocols and software that presents information in a hypertext format.

While the adoption of Transmission Control Protocol/Internet Protocol (TCP/IP) resulted in the rapid expansion of the Internet, another individual, Tim Berners-Lee, and others at the European Laboratory for Particle Physics, more popularly known as CERN, proposed a new protocol for information distribution. Scientists at CERN were struggling to find a way to share a huge variety of documents, ranging from experimental data to computer documentation to up-to-the-minute news of scientific breakthroughs, with the large community of physicists who could benefit from such access. What evolved from this is hypertext.

10.1 Hypertext

Tim Berners-Lee first conceived of the protocols that make it possible for Web documents to be accessible to desktop computers around the world. In a note to his colleagues at CERN, he shared his perception of a need:

> The current incompatibilities of the platforms and tools make it impossible to access existing information through a common interface, leading to waste of time, frustration, and obsolete answers to simple data lookup. There is a potential large benefit from the integration of a variety of systems in a way which allows a user to follow links pointing from one piece of information to another one (Berners-Lee, and Cailliau).

G. O'Toole, *Sustainable Web Ecosystem Design,*
SpringerBriefs in Computer Science, DOI: 10.1007/978-1-4614-7714-3_10,
© The Author(s) 2013

The result was HyperText, a system of embedding links in text that link to other text. The WWW was created under the assumption that many people would be able to work collaboratively by putting information on a web of hypertext documents.

Tim Berners-Lee made several contributions to the development of the Internet, from his work on hypertext and protocols to helping develop the World Wide Web. These contributions help standardize methods of displaying and exchanging data over the Internet. Without the development of TCP/IP protocols and hypertext, the public may not have adopted the Internet in the same manner it is accepted today.

10.2 Hypertext Transfer Protocol

The subsequent protocol developed, Hypertext Transfer Protocol (HTTP), simplified the writing of addresses, automatically searched the Internet for the address indicated, and automatically called up the document for viewing. For decades prior to the Web, access to computers and computer networks was through text-only terminals or terminal emulator programs.

The first web browser, a line-mode browser that could only run on text-only, VT 100 terminals, was developed by Berners-Lee and released to the public in 1991. Berners-Lee coined the name World Wide Web as a name for the program. WWW could be put on servers, and the browser would allow one to access the information stored on the server.

10.3 HyperText Markup Language (HTML)

HyperText Markup Language (HTML) is the main language used to create Web pages, reaching a current version of 5.0. HTML 5 is still in its infancy, and most web pages today conform to the HTML 4.01 standard and eXtensible HyperText Markup Language (XHTML) standard, its successor. XHTML addresses the shortcomings of HTML 4.01 by allowing developers to easily embrace future changes and display devices. XHTML also renders (displays) with more consistency on different browsers and display devices.

There are two main flavors of XHTML, transitional and strict. Many developers use transitional XHTML, as it's more forgiving of coding errors than strict XHTML. It also includes some backward compatibility with older versions of HTML, so when you change a Web page from HTML to XHTML it is less likely to malfunction. Think of it as the next step beyond HTML 4.01. The most recent version of HTML is HTML 5. This robust language includes a wide use of JavaScript and other additions and refinements to the language.[1]

10.4 Document Object Model

The document object model is a standard for displaying the structure of code that is behind the scenes of each one of your Web pages. The DOM affects HTML, XHTML, and XML code. The document part of this term pertains to the Web page itself. You can call this a file, a page, or a document. They all mean pretty much the same thing in this context. The object in this term pertains to the pieces of the document. The parts of the code, the different tags, and each of the content items in the page are all pieces of the document. The model in this term pertains to an agreed upon set of terms, that is, the conventional way of displaying the page and all of its parts. Without a DOM, or document object model in place, the Web simply would not work the way it does now.

> The Document Object Model is a platform- and language-neutral interface that will allow programs and scripts to dynamically access and update the content, structure and style of documents. The document can be further processed and the results of that processing can be incorporated back into the presented page. (Le Hégaret)

JavaScript can be used to manipulate the DOM. The DOM is intertwined with the history of the conflicts of various Web browsers and the versioning they each have gone through in their history. Different Web browsers use different layout engines (for more see http://en.wikipedia.org/wiki/List_of_web_browsers), but the important thing to remember here is that Web browsers rely on layout engines to parse HTML into a DOM.

For quick reference, the DOM breaks down something like this:

Document = Web page

Object = Piecesend

Model = Agreed upon set of terms

10.5 Web Browsers

Web designers and authors are in agreement that the toughest challenges related to Web design center around the issues of multiple browsers and platforms. This is an enormous problem since each browser or platform has distinct characteristics that

---

[1] HTML 5 includes many additions and refinements to the language, about which many books have already been written. Additionally, there are many useful and updated Web references for further learning about HTML 5. More information can be found at http://www.w3.org/html/wg/drafts/html/master.

will impact the appearance of the site. If everyone had the same platform and browser, there would be few problems. But, unfortunately, that is not the case.

Browsers are software programs that view Web pages and help you move through the Web. The browser that triggered the WWW explosion was Mosaic, a public domain graphical user interface (GUI) from the National Center for Supercomputer Applications (NCSA). Released in 1993, Mosaic made it possible to design documents containing images for display over the Internet. Up to that point, an Internet document was basically just a bunch of text on a server.

Four browsers dominate the market today: Firefox (a Mozilla-based browser), Microsoft Internet Explorer, Google Chrome, and Apple Safari. Thus, competition between these four companies has continued the rapid development of browser technologies as each try to establish dominance. While this has been positive for the rapid proliferation of the Internet to the customer, it has caused serious compatibility issues as vendors try to outdo the competition. Unfortunately, because of this fierce competition, vendors have developed proprietary technologies to establish an edge on the competition without adhering to international standard initiatives.

The following information will serve as a background and hopefully provide some guidance to inform the design process. Remember that because there are so many variables, there is no single solution. It will depend entirely on your audience, design criteria, and purpose of your Web site.

10.5.1 Background

In 1993 Marc Andreessen of the NCSA (National Center for SuperComputing Applications, Illinois) launched Mosaic X. This browser was released to the public on X, PC, Windows, and Macintosh platforms and was an immediate hit. It was easy to install, easy to use, and enormously improved the graphic capabilities of the Web. Mosaic made it possible for users with direct or dialup Internet connections to navigate through the Web viewing multimedia documents, complete with different fonts, styled text, and inline graphics. By 1994 tens of thousands of versions had been installed on computers throughout the world. The potential of HTML to create graphically attractive Web sites, and the ease with which these sites could be accessed through the new generations of Web browsers, opened the Web to whole new groups. These developments were accelerated by the appearance of ever more powerful and affordable personal computers and by the increase in capacity of the communications infrastructure. These developments led to the rapid expansion of the WWW.

In April 1994, Marc Andreessen, who conceived and spearheaded the development of Mosaic, left the NCSA to co-found Mosaic Communications in Mountain View, California. (The company changed its name to Netscape Communications in November of that year). In October 1994, the first version of Netscape Navigator was made available on the Internet and was the most successful graphical type of browser and server until Microsoft declared war and developed its Microsoft Internet Explorer. At the end of 1995, Microsoft realized the rising importance of the Internet and committed itself to establishing dominance in the Web browser market.

Compared to the available versions of Netscape, the first two releases of Internet Explorer were uneventful. However, the release of Internet Explorer 3.0 in August 1996, and its subsequent incorporation into future versions of the Windows operating system, signified Microsoft's first serious entry into the World Wide Web browser market. According to one source, as of December of 2012, roughly 15 % of users are using IE, 31 % are using Firefox, and 46 % are using Chrome, and just over 4 % are using Safari. Thus Chrome has become the dominant browser (W3C Schools).

There are a variety of other popular browsers that account for the rest of the browser market. In addition, the emergence of the iPad and other tablet computers, as well as smart phones such as the iPhone, Android and Blackberry, has complicated the target for the Web designer. Because of this it is important that designers and developers try to stay focused on W3C recommendations, and to conduct tests on a variety of browsers and platforms to be aware of where their sites may differ or fail to deliver the desired content. The important idea here is that Web designers and developers need to consider their intended audience, obtain information on the most likely browsers for that audience and design and develop for the least common denominator in terms of browser compatibility. This will also let the designer/developer estimate the potential audience for their web site based on the browser usage statistics that are available online.

10.5.2 Popular Web Browser Descriptions

Included here is a short list of popular Web browsers. Depending on your type of computer, tablet, or mobile device, your personal preferences, and other variables certain Web browsers may be better suited to your needs. This is certainly not an exhaustive list, and your own needs should be assessed during your research for the most fitting Web browser for you. (For more see http://en.wikipedia.org/wiki/List_of_web_browsers).

Apple Safari—This is the Web browser that comes installed on all Apple Mac computers and mobile devices. Apple claims that Safari is 100 % compliant with current Web standards.

Opera—Opera is a marvelous Web client from Norway. The browser is fast, small, powerful, and very user-friendly. The creators of this browser claim it is faster, more secure, and more customizable than any other browser. It is ideal for visually impaired Web surfers and Web researchers. Many designers use this browser for testing how well their HTML is produced. Versions are available in English, German, Norwegian, Spanish, Afrikaans, Italian and French.

Lynx—Lynx is a text-only, freely distributed browser that focuses on delivering the minimum standard for Web page delivery. Lynx has been the browser of choice for displaying text only information on hand-held devices that have little or no graphic display capability.

Amaya—Amaya is the name of World Wide Web Consortium's (W3C) own browser/authoring tool and is used to demonstrate and test many of the new developments in Web protocols and data formats. Both versatile and extensible, the application is available on Unix, Windows, and Macintosh platforms. (See http://www.w3.org/Amaya).

Google Chrome—Google boasts minimal design with sophisticated technology to make the Web faster, safer, and easier.

Smartphone Browsers—These browsers are designed for use on smartphones, such as the Apple iPhone. Examples include Google Chrome, Opera Mini, and Safari.

10.6 Accessibility

Accessibility guidelines put in place by the U.S. Federal Government are recommendations on how to make information technology fairly accessible by all people with disabilities. A prime resource is the U.S. Government Web site on Section 508 of the Americans With Disabilities Act. Additionally, there many other considerations in sustainable Web ecosystem design which fall under the accessibility header.

10.6.1 The Limitations of the Users' Computer Systems[2]

How fast is the average user's connection? Keep in mind that if your design computer has a T1 connection to the Internet, a streaming video that plays fine off your design computer may stutter, skip frames, or not even play at all for most users who have a 56K modem connection to the Internet. For this reason, many site designers today have developed a minimalist philosophy—give just enough information. If something like streaming video is crucial to your site, make the users aware of the problems they may encounter, and try to offer some alternatives (such as still pictures with an audio-only overlay, or perhaps just a text overlay).

What browser will the typical user run? What plug-ins do users have? Keep in mind having to download a new browser and plug-ins over a modem connection is

---

[2] This information came from Penn State's Teaching and Learning with Technology: http://tlt.psu.edu/suggestions/accessibility/css.html, Accessed 5-14-08.

usually an interruption. This may discourage users from even looking at your site. Some sites proclaim what browser the site was designed on and for. Use of good, clean HTML can partially avoid browser incompatibilities. The important thing here is to test your pages prior to release on all possible browsers and systems you believe your users will run.

Accessibility is about making sure a site reaches everyone who wants to be reached, and particularly addresses the special user who has some disability that limits his/her ability to access information on the Web, if those needs haven't been considered and addressed. Remember that there are 40 million Americans who have disabilities. If that percentage were consistent, that would make the number of disabled worldwide 1,000,000,000. Chances are that the number is greater than that. The Web is increasingly reaching people worldwide, especially in the most populous nations of the world, China and India.

It is often pointed out that access to education is the way out of poverty and deprivation. The disabled are the largest group in most societies who are denied an education. The Web can address that if developers take the time to make sure a site is available and accessible to those individuals who possess a disability. This is central to education; that it is also central to sales may need to be pointed out. If customers can find the product and information about it, they may buy it.

To check the usability of your Web site, you can turn to the Web itself for assistance. Here are some links to sites that provide information and ways to check your sites.

10.6.2 The Limitations of the User

All sites should be accessible to users who have a variety of different limitations. Currently most sites are not. What is called for is careful and thoughtful preparation and coding of a site. Here is a checklist of things that should be done when preparing a Web site to make it easier for those with disabilities. The percentage of people with disabilities who are on the Web is greater than those without—it is a fine way to level the learning and work environments so all can enter, but it requires care and thoughtfulness.

- What disabilities limit users' access to information, like images or colors? For instance, 10 % of men are red/green colorblind. Using this combination of colors in a foreground/background scheme would be disastrous.
- Can your user follow along and understand long sentences? Dyslexics cannot.
- Are the distinctions made in color and shape great enough to be seen by the user? It is important to realize that as people get older, they often can make fewer subtle distinctions of color and shape.

• Does your user have use of his/her basic motor functions—can s/he use a mouse to navigate your site by pointing, clicking, and dragging? In the United States alone, we need to serve more than 40 million people with disabilities and currently about 75 % of them use the Web (50 % of the general population do).

The virtual world of the Web, just like physical public buildings, need to be accessible to people with disabilities. For example, special machines have been created to allow visually impaired individuals to access the Internet through special braille devices and readers. As developers, we need to be aware of this and try to accommodate these special individuals by using certain tags that help make pages more accessible. Accessibility is a necessary node that must be considered when mapping the anatomy of sustainable Web ecosystem design.

Suggested Web Resource(s):

Penn State's Web Accessibility Project: http://accessibility.psu.edu/
W3C Web accessibility tools: http://www.w3.org/WAI/ER/tools/complete
US Government Section 508 Online: http://www.section508.gov
Jeffery Zeldman: http://www.zeldman.com/category/w3c

10.7 Universality

Cross-platform, cross-browser, and operating system agnostic are a few terms being used widely. The basic idea here is to make your project universal in respect to the environments in which it will work. Universality is a necessary node that must be considered when mapping the anatomy of sustainable Web ecosystem design.

10.8 Searchability

Once users arrive at your product and start using it, you want them to be able to find exactly what they are looking for. Searchability is a necessary node that must be considered when mapping the anatomy of sustainable Web ecosystem design. This can also map back to being an important part of usability. Flexibility in the ways your users utilize your project is very important. Don't limit the user to being able to do things only one way. They won't stay long.

10.9 Scalability

How big is your project now? How big will it be in a year, 5 years, how about ten? Scalable architecture is a necessary node that must be considered when mapping the anatomy of sustainable Web ecosystem design.

Suggested Web Resource(s):

The Art of Scalability: http://theartofscalability.com

10.10 Social-Sharing

By default users of the Web today expect social functionality in what they do. You need to decide which social media channels will you support on your site and from your site. Social-sharing is a necessary node that must be considered when mapping the anatomy of sustainable Web ecosystem design.

10.11 Responsiveness

By default users of the Web today expect social functionality in what they do. Responsive Web Design (RWD) of a site is a necessary node that must be considered when mapping the anatomy of sustainable Web ecosystem design. In the old days, on introductory pages to Web sites, designers often indicated at what resolution the site is best viewed. This was a good practice if you felt that the site would have a wide variety of users with varied monitor sizes and resolution settings. When conducting an audience analysis, try to determine at what level most end users set their monitor resolutions.

As a Web designer, you will discover that nothing can cause more frustration than seeing your design look totally different on someone else's computer. Browsers and individual user preferences (fonts, size, color, etc.) can play a significant role in this appearance. But display technology also has an equally important role in the look of your designs when they are made public. Understanding the importance of display devices and their characteristics can contribute greatly to the success of your site.

The following information will look at how site design directions can be influenced by display technologies and viewing conditions. Two characteristics of displays that have major implications for Web designers are monitor size (resolution) and color depth (number of displayable colors, although with contemporary monitor technology, this is rarely an issue anymore). But these are not the only considerations that site designers must think about during the development of a

Web site. Designers must also address a whole new spectrum of devices that are becoming more popular as our society gets much more mobile.

Suggested Web Resource(s):

Responsive Web Design on Wikipedia: http://en.wikipedia.org/wiki/Responsive_web_design

Suggested Book(s):

Responsive Web Design by Ethan Marcotte: http://www.abookapart.com/products/responsive-web-design
Mobile First by Luke Wroblewski: http://www.abookapart.com/products/mobile-first

10.12 Testing

No matter if this is your first site or your twentieth, testing is vital to the design of your finished product. Testing will give you an opportunity to put your site through the paces and determine problems before it is released to the public. It is important to look at your site through a variety of browsers and under different load circumstances at key points in the development process. The more media elements you use, the higher the load, and the more potential problems. This process will ensure that the site operates successfully and without major problems.

There are two basic techniques you should use when testing a site under development: Observation and Think-alouds. Allow users similar to your target audience to test early (alpha) and more mature but not finalized (beta) versions of your site while you watch them. You may also ask them to think aloud as they do so. Capturing their actions, motions, and words can greatly aid you in clearing up confusing issues and streamlining the user experience. You should also run as many site validation checks as possible.

Suggested Web Resource(s):

Adobe Browser Labs: http://browserlab.adobe.com
Browser Shots.org: http://browsershots.org/
Cross Browser Testing: http://crossbrowsertesting.com/
Multiple validators: http://www.webnauts.net/check.html

Chapter 11
Image

Let's face it; if a Web ecosystem is not entertaining, you won't have users sticking around very long. The image has captivated humanity, and certainly those of us on this side of the access digital divide. Image is a necessary node that must be considered when mapping the anatomy of sustainable Web ecosystem design.

11.1 Data Visualization

As we enter into a new era of big data, we must be innovative in the ways in which we mine, browse, and present our data so that it is most efficiently presented to our viewers. Whether you are working with data sets or other types of information, creating maps, graphs, charts, or dynamic interfaces as part of the Web, data visualization is a huge field today and is a necessary node that must be considered when mapping the anatomy of sustainable Web ecosystem design.

11.2 Multi-Formats

JPG, GIF, TIFF, PNG, BMP. What are they, and how do you choose? Several different graphic file formats currently exist, with many more formats in testing. Certain types of images, like photographs with lots of different colors, should be saved as a certain graphic format, line art and logos, for example, should be saved and used in another format. By knowing the different characteristics of each graphic format, you can correctly choose how to best save your graphics files. These and many other file types are used to encode digital images. The choices are simpler than you might think.

Part of the reason for the plethora of file types is the need for compression. Image files can be quite large, and larger file types mean more disk usage and slower downloads. Compression is a term used to describe ways of cutting the size

G. O'Toole, *Sustainable Web Ecosystem Design*,
SpringerBriefs in Computer Science, DOI: 10.1007/978-1-4614-7714-3_11,

of the file. Compression schemes can by "lossy" or "lossless" depending on whether or not image quality in the form of pixelated information is lost or retained. Another reason for the many file types is that images differ in the number of colors they contain. If an image has few colors, a file type can be designed to exploit this as a way of reducing file size.

11.2.1 Definitions of Basic Terms

Resolution: The quality (sharpness, clarity) of an image. Resolution is qualitative as well as quantitative and is measured in terms of ppi and dpi.

PPI: (pixels per inch) Measurement used for images displayed on screen.

DPI: (dots per inch) Measurement used in printing images.

Pixel: A word invented from "picture element"—the basic unit of programmable color on a computer display or in a computer image.

Megapixel: A megapixel (that is, a million pixels) is a unit of image sensing capacity in a digital camera. In general, the more megapixels in a camera, the better the resolution when printing an image in a given size.

Lossy: A term meaning "with losses," used to describe image file formats that discard data due to compression.

Lossless: A term used to describe an image file format that retains all the data from the initial image file.

RGB: (Red, Green, Blue) The color model for display devices (monitors, digital projectors, etc.) Each displayed color is determined by a combination of RGB.

CMYK: (Cyan, Magenta, Yellow, and Black) The color model for printing.

Bit-mapped (or Raster) images: Images that have data that describe the color of each pixel. Larger display sizes equal larger file sizes in this type of image. Bitmapped images cannot be rescaled without resulting in "pixilation", or loss of definition in the details. JPEG and GIF images are examples of bitmapped images.

Vector images: Vector images have data that describe lines and curves. These images can be enlarged and still maintain their smooth edges (not pixilated like bitmap images). Artists and designers will often work with vector images, and then "rasterize" the finalized version for distribution and display. Adobe Illustrator files (.ai) and CorelDraw files (.cdr) are examples of vector images.

Proprietary: Denotes ownership and nondisclosure of details regarding format or programming code. In the context of images, proprietary refers to file formats that require a certain software application to read/open that file. For example, .psd is the proprietary file format for native Adobe Photoshop files.

Open Source: Denotes a more accessible way to share, improve and distribute resources, requiring that licensing not be specific to a particular product.

It is also helpful to understand the common image file formats of digital images, how these file formats differ, and what their recommended use is. TIFF (.tif), JPG (.jpg, .jpeg), GIF (.gif) and PNG (.png) are file formats (and their respective file extensions) that you are likely to encounter. Other image file formats are used to a lesser extent; these formats are often proprietary, such as Photoshop.psd files.

TIFF: A lossless file format that can be compressed. This format is widely supported across operating systems. TIFF is the best file format for archiving high quality images.

JPG or JPEG: The JPG file format was specifically created for photographs, and can contain millions of colors. JPGs are automatically compressed (you can choose the level of compression to match your desired image quality), resulting in a relatively small file size while still retaining quality. For this reason, JPGs are ideal for email and Web use. JPGs are lossy, discarding information each time that they are compressed.

GIF: The lossless and compressed file format that is preferred for graphics, because it keeps edges and lines sharp. GIFs are limited to 256 or fewer colors, and are not recommended for photographs, but rather for images with flat fields of color, such as clip art. GIFs can be static or animated.

PNG: Portable Network Graphics format, an open source substitute for GIFs. PNGs provide a higher lossless compression rate than GIFs, and help to reduce cross-platform differences in image display quality, among other technical advantages. PNG provides a useful format for the storage of images during intermediate stages of editing.

All of the formats detailed above are readable in both Windows and Mac OS operating systems, and are supported by most image viewing and editing applications.

Computer display resolution: Images intended primarily for display on a computer monitor (such as email attachments or images on a Web page) really only need a 72 ppi to 96 ppi resolution, as that is what computer monitors are capable of displaying. A higher resolution will not make your image appear any better on the screen. In fact, if you don't expect folks to print out your images, these images should be "optimized", which means making them as small and compressed a file as possible (while still retaining the appropriate visual clarity), so that they load quickly, and do not take up too much space on the hard drive. Apple's recent Retina Display technology resolutions are much higher. For example, the most recent iPad displays up to 264 ppi, and the iPhone: 326 ppi. These will certainly increase in the near future.

11.3 Dynamic Interface

A dynamic interface can fall in many sub-nodes of the anatomy of sustainable Web ecosystem design. We can talk about it in many ways, not the least important of which image. The interface of a project forms the totality of the composition. We may use images and video in a single Web page or a scalable vector graphic in one screen of a mobile app, but the entire user area acts as one singular image. This "image" must be dynamic. Dynamic interface is a necessary node that must be considered when mapping the anatomy of sustainable Web ecosystem design.

The web is interactive, filled with dynamic websites where you can pull in data on the fly, cause pages to change based on your actions, and add data to a site. This differs from static websites, which primarily consist of text and graphics you can only read and view. In this topic, we will explain the differences between dynamic and static websites, as well as give you a basic understanding of some different methods to include interactivity in a website.

Originally called LiveScript, JavaScript is a cross-platform, object-oriented scripting language created by Brendan Eich of Netscape. JavaScript consists of two components—Client-side JavaScript, and Server-side JavaScript. Core JavaScript is the combination of both client and server-side JavaScript. Core JavaScript encompasses all of the statements, operators, objects, and functions that make up the basic JavaScript language. This lesson will discuss core JavaScript, calling it simply "JavaScript." (Please note that Java and JavaScript are two entirely different things).

JavaScript allows the web page developer to add some interactivity and conditional behavior to web pages. Using JavaScript code you can add functionality and interactivity to your HTML and CSS code. You may have the need to create mouse rollover effects on buttons, text, and images; make forms interactive; display additional information about links; create pop-up messages; change the contents of pages based on certain conditions; create and load content into new browser windows; and/or perform calculations and manipulations on text and numbers. This is by no means an exhaustive list of what you can accomplish with JavaScript; it is merely a list of the most common things JavaScript is used to accomplish. There are literally thousands of JavaScript examples that exist today, and you can write your own as well.

There are advantages to using JavaScript. JavaScripts are scripted commands, that is, text statements usually embedded in the section of an HTML document. Thus, JavaScript loads when the page does, and loads quite quickly and can be stored in a library file and called by HTML documents. Once JavaScript loads, calls back to the server are (usually) not required. This allows the web page to dynamically respond to the user with no additional signal traffic. Dozens of JavaScript libraries containing thousands of JavaScript examples are available on the web, making it easy to find a script that either meets your needs or can be easily adapted to meet your needs. Most of these scripts are in the public domain.

There are advantages to using JavaScript. For example, anyone can see the JavaScript source code by viewing the HTML document source. Thus you could not create a secure multiple-choice test in JavaScript; it would be very easy to see the answers. Even though JavaScript is a standard, different browsers interpret JavaScript differently, and some commands that work fine on one browser simply do not work on another. You must carefully test your JavaScript code on all browsers to make sure it runs correctly. If someone turns JavaScript off (via their Preferences), your script(s) will not execute. People may do this for several reasons. Have you ever closed a window in a browser, only to have another one appear? Or visited a site where windows start popping up all over the place? Usually these windows are created by using JavaScript. Turn JavaScript off and the "problem" goes away. Another reason people turn JavaScript off is to prevent client-side setting of Cookies, tiny files that store information about you.

There are several reasons to include JavaScript. JavaScript can add interactivity to a web page, from fairly passive mouse rollovers to aggressive form validation. If you have the need for such interactive capabilities, you should consider JavaScript in relation to competing technologies, such as CGI scripts and Java applets. If you are not concerned about people viewing the script's source code, and JavaScript can accomplish the task for you on the browsers and platforms you must work with, then it is the recommended choice, for it reduces traffic to and from the server. If security is an issue, then JavaScript must be discarded in favor of more secure environments, such as CGI scripts or Java applets.

11.4 Image Genome

Images, like living creatures, have a genomic pattern to them. They are the root characteristics that, when culminating on the surface of an image, make viewable the personality of the image. We may not see the image genome. What we see is the surface of the image that directly constitutes the qualities of a painting, photograph or logo that we like or dislike. These qualities can bring multiple images together or set them apart. It is desirable to have unification of images in our projects that can lead directly to an aesthetic appeal for the user. As we know, the user experience is very important, and the images we choose to use, and how they relate to the other visual characters on the interactive stage, play a key role in the quality of this user experience. Genome is a necessary node that must be considered when mapping the anatomy of sustainable Web ecosystem design.

Suggested Web Resource(s):

W3C Responsive Images Group: http://www.w3.org/community/respimg
W3 Schools HTML Images: http://www.w3schools.com/html/html_images.asp
James Wang Research, IST PSU: http://wang.ist.psu.edu/docs/home.shtml
Jeffery Zeldman: http://www.zeldman.com/category/w3c

Chapter 12
Writing

Although you may utilize fascinating video and other interactive mixed media content, you cannot get away with less than stellar written word if your site is going to succeed. Not only does the writing need to be accessible, interesting, accurate and well written, factors of consistency, tone, personality, and a common voice all play into the effectiveness of your writing. This section focuses on the written word as yet another a necessary node that must be considered when mapping the anatomy of sustainable Web ecosystem design.

12.1 Creative

Your writing must be creative. You won't run into the need to write many book-length articles on your site, and you probably won't have to write too much original laborious scientific research. You will most likely have brief passages that help the user navigate around or find out more about what it s you are presenting. Whatever you write, make it creative. It's your space to make the content interesting, so do so. Show off some personality. The creative approach to (at least some of) your written content is a necessary node that must be considered when mapping the anatomy of sustainable Web ecosystem design.

12.2 Technical

Technical writing in this case usually has to do with any instructional documentation your site may contain. It is common to have tutorial or "how-to" type content on a Web site. Technical writing that may be of use to your target audience is a necessary node that must be considered when mapping the anatomy of sustainable Web ecosystem design.

G. O'Toole, *Sustainable Web Ecosystem Design*,
SpringerBriefs in Computer Science, DOI: 10.1007/978-1-4614-7714-3_12,
© The Author(s) 2013

12.3 Documentary

Web app sections such as About Us, Organization History, News, Events, and product evaluations and reviews are all types of documentary writing. This, too, is a necessary node that must be considered when mapping the anatomy of sustainable Web ecosystem design.

12.4 Critical

In writing content for a news documentary application consider the impact of accessing news of the day where individuals have to deal with "spin," the added layer of subjectivity to fact. In accessing news, that is, being a news consumer while trying to gain information and understand the events of our world, spin can be a real speed bump. To make matters worse, then there is "hype." How do individuals navigate through the hottest story of the day? The more you look into postmodern information theory, the more you see that at this late stage of the game, there are no centers from which to stand and make an objectively informed judgment.

Today's news organizations are posters for exploiting the spectacle. During the O.J. Simpson "white Bronco" event of 1994, as an example, 95 million (Linder) television viewers tuned in. When the trial was over 142 million people listened on radio and watched television as the verdict was delivered, an astounding 91 % of television viewers. Some say this was the event that took television news shows and magazines from the role of news informer to newsmaker and created a new genre of television content: Infotainment. Although this may make the news more fun to consume, in considering the dilemma, this type of news coverage overloads the viewer with content.

What some of these shows are good for is having an obsessive operation of posting and broadcasting enormous amounts of coverage on what is happening around the world, and using new and innovative methods of dissemination and delivery. Whether all of this content is necessary or relevant is another topic. This high quantity of data is not all bad, all of it is information, importantly though there is an outlet for everyone nowadays, no matter what an audience member's point of view is. Critical thought and expression is a necessary node that must be considered when mapping the anatomy of sustainable Web ecosystem design.

Chapter 13
Code

Writing proper, valid HTML, and any code for that matter, is vital to ensure that the pages, the site, and/or the applications being developed work successfully and will continue to work successfully over time. To make sure that your code is properly formed, several approaches can be used. The two most common approaches are validation services to check your Web site, or development tools to check your code for accuracy.

Several validation services have opened shop on the Internet to check Web sites for code quality issues. These validation services will check HTML for errors and provide a report. Some services are free, while others charge for the service. Alternatively, many popular HTML authoring tools now incorporate built-in features that allow coders to check their work. One such tool is Adobe's Dreamweaver. By using the "Check Target Browser" feature, designers can specify which browser they would like to target in their site design. This browser is then opened and HTML is displayed. Dreamweaver then checks to see if the HTML is appropriate for the browser specified. Valid code is a necessary node that must be considered when mapping the anatomy of sustainable Web ecosystem design.

Suggested Web Resource(s):

W3C HTML Validation Service: http://validator.w3.org

13.1 Stability Through Standards

Validating your code will ensure stability over time. To work within the proper and established Web standards helps to this end. The W3C or World Wide Web Consortium is the Web standards leader as an international community that develops open standards to ensure the long-term growth of the Web. The W3C standards "define an Open Web Platform for application development that has the unprecedented potential to enable developers to build rich interactive experiences,

G. O'Toole, *Sustainable Web Ecosystem Design*,
SpringerBriefs in Computer Science, DOI: 10.1007/978-1-4614-7714-3_13,
© The Author(s) 2013

powered by vast data stores, that are available on any device." (W3.org) Incorporating this stability into your Web projects is a necessary node that must be considered when mapping the anatomy of sustainable Web ecosystem design.

Suggested Web Resource(s):

W3C Web Standards: http://www.w3.org/standards.

13.2 Lightweight

It is always important when creating Web content of all kinds to consider the "weight" of the material you are putting on your server. Another way of thinking about the weight is the term bandwidth. The total weight of your files, or the bandwidth, is the size of the files along with the types of files, which take a certain amount of time to transfer from the Web server to the users screen. For example, say you are sharing a weekend trip you took with some friends over the Web. If you have Web page with four jpgs, one mpg, and some text explaining your adventure, you would essentially have six elements that need to download from your Web server to each of your friends computers or devices when they went to view your material. You would have

$$1 \text{ html file} + 4 \text{ images} + 1 \text{ video} = 6 \text{ total elements.}$$

Incidentally, these six files would show up as six independent "hits" in your analytics software. To optimize this experience for your friends, you would want to make this site as lightweight as possible. In other words you would want to use the least amount of bandwidth that would be possible while maintaining the highest quality experience you can offer to your friends and anyone else who may see your site. There are many ways of going about this optimization process from streaming audio and video media instead of downloading to using media queries to server up the best content based on users bandwidth. Lightweight Web experiences for all of your users are a necessary node that must be considered when mapping the anatomy of sustainable Web ecosystem design.

Suggested Web Resource(s):

Google Developers Speed: https://developers.google.com/speed
Steve Sounders, Head Performance Engineer at Google: http://www.stevesouders.com/blog/2012/02/10/the-performance-golden-rule

Suggested Book(s):

High Performance Web Sites: Essential Knowledge for Front-End Engineers, by Steve Sounders, O'Reilly Media.

13.3 Secure

Security is always a top concern in anything you do on the Web. Taking smart, tested steps to ensure your code for your project is safe and secure is a necessary node that must be considered when mapping the anatomy of sustainable Web ecosystem design. The issue of Web security is a living issue, which means, like most of the Web, it is constantly evolving, changing, and being updated for any number of reasons. Technologies improve, risks increase, and, thankfully, methods of securing our sites also improve. There is no way to sum up the topic of Web code security in one simple missive. The best thing you can do to make your sites and your code safe and secure is to start learning now, and make it a habit of checking several of the top sites that offer updated methodologies on Web security.

Suggested Web Resource(s):

Mozilla Guidelines: https://wiki.mozilla.org/WebAppSec/Secure_Coding_Guide
lines
Google Code: http://code.google.com/edu/security/index.html[1]
Google Developers: https://developers.google.com

13.4 Open

The term open source describes practices in production and development that promote access to the end product's source materials. Some consider open source a philosophy, others consider it a pragmatic methodology. Before the term open source became widely adopted, developers and producers used a variety of phrases to describe the concept; open source gained hold with the rise of the Internet, and the attendant need for massive retooling of the computing source code. Opening the source code enabled a self-enhancing diversity of production models, com-munication paths, and interactive communities. Subsequently, the new phrase "open-source software" was born to describe the environment that the new copyright, licensing, domain, and consumer issues created. The open source model includes the concept of concurrent yet different agendas and differing approaches in production, in contrast with more centralized models of development such as those typically used in commercial software companies. A main principle and practice of open source software development is peer production by bartering and collaboration, with the end-product, source-material, "blueprints," and docu-mentation available at no cost to the public.

---

[1] Google Code is currently in transition. Other useful resources here are https://developers.google.com and https://developers.google.com/university.

The philosophy and development model of open source is a method for creating software that "harnesses the power of distributed peer review and transparency of process" with the goal of "better quality, higher reliability, more flexibility, lower cost, and an end to predatory vendor lock-in."

The Open Source Initiative, one leading open source advocate organizations is involved in creating a "standards body, maintaining the Open Source Definition for the good of the community." Open source goes way beyond just making your code available for others to use, and it is a necessary node that must be considered when mapping the anatomy of sustainable Web ecosystem design.

Suggested Web Resource(s):

Open Source Initiative (OSI): http://opensource.org
Open Source Definition: http://opensource.org/docs/osd
Open Source.com: http://opensource.com/resources/what-open-source.

13.4.1 Semantic

The basic meaning of the word "semantic" is "meaning". What we mean when we talk about the Semantic Web is that we give objects meaning so that not just people can understand the information that is the Web, but so that computers can also understand the information that is the Web. To get a historical perspective here we can look at the dominant characteristics of the Web over time (Table 13.1).

The semantic standard is largely encouraged by the W3C. The standard promotes common data formats on the World Wide Web. There are several widely used data formats for semantic code.

Microformats are simple ways to add information to a web page using mostly the class attribute (although sometimes the id, title, rel orrev attributes too). The class names are semantically rich and describe the data they encapsulate.

With RDFa (Resource Description Framework in attributes), a W3C recommendation, you can easily include extra "structure" in your (X)HTML to indicate a calendar event, contact information, a document license, etc. RDFa is about total publisher control: you choose which attributes to use, which to reuse from other sites, and how to evolve, over time, the meaning of these attributes.

The OWL Web Ontology Language is designed for use by applications that need to process the content of information instead of just presenting information to humans. OWL facilitates greater machine interpretability of Web content than that supported by XML, RDF, and RDF Schema (RDF-S) by providing additional vocabulary along with a formal semantics. OWL has three increasingly-expressive sublanguages: OWL Lite, OWL DL, and OWL Full.

The Dublin Core Metadata Initiative, or "DCMI," is an open organization engaged in the development of interoperable metadata standards that support a broad range of purposes and business models. DCMI's activities include work on

Table 13.1 The dominant characteristics of the "versions" of the Web to date

Web "version"	Approximate years	Traits
Web 1.0	1994–1999	Code heavy
		Static
		Bottlenecks
		Webmasters only
Web 2.0	2000–2008	User generated content
		Tags
		Dynamic, data driven
Web 3.0	2009–present	Semantic
		Usability/user psychology
		Software as service
		Cloud computing
		Mobility/ubiquitous
		Augmented reality
		Micro-payments
		Open source
		CMS

architecture and modeling, discussions and collaborative work in DCMI Communities and DCMI Task Groups, annual conferences and workshops, standards liaison, and educational efforts to promote widespread acceptance of metadata standards and practices.

Coding for semantic understanding is a necessary node that must be considered when mapping the anatomy of sustainable Web ecosystem design.

Suggested Web Resource(s):

Microformats: http://microformats.org
RDFa: http://rdfa.info
W3C Semantic Web Ontology Language OWL: http://www.w3.org/TR/owl-features
Dublin Core Metadata Initiative: http://dublincore.org.

13.5 Interoperable

For our purposes here, the quality of interoperability is considered to be a type of compatibility. "Interoperability is a property of a product or system, whose interfaces are completely understood, to work with other products or systems, present or future, without any restricted access or implementation" (Wikipedia). The IEEE defines interoperable as "the ability of two or more systems or components to exchange information and to use the information that has been exchanged." This efficiency of code and all other Web elements is a necessary node that must be considered when mapping the anatomy of sustainable Web ecosystem design.

13.6 Energy Utilization

The W3C hosts a Web Protocols and Energy Utilization Community Group. The purpose of the group is to create a space for brainstorming and collaborating on the problem of lowering the necessary energy consumption of Web protocols, that is, the data transferring mechanisms that make the Web possible. At present there is not much activity within the forums, however there are many great initiatives, ideas, and blog posts on the Web that are starting to address and come up with solutions for Internet energy consumption. This consideration of energy efficiency whether it is for the good of the environment or the good of the user experience is a necessary node that must be considered when mapping the anatomy of sustainable Web ecosystem design.

Suggested Web Resource(s):

W3C Web Protocols and Energy Utilization: http://www.w3.org/community/web protoenergy
W3C WPEUG Willy Svenningsson Partial Serving of XHTML demo: http://www.deciweb.se/SuggestionsW3C
Net Magazine article by Pete Markiewicz: http://www.netmagazine.com/features/save-planet-through-sustainable-web-design
Pete Markiewicz, Green Resources, Energy Use Optimization: http://sustainablevirtualdesign.wordpress.com.

Chapter 14
Web Hosting

Where your project resides is an important element to any successful operation. A project is a system and all parts of that system count. Hosting is a necessary node that must be considered when mapping the anatomy of sustainable Web ecosystem design.

Nearly all web pages are delivered in the same, basic way. A remote server (it can be anywhere in the world) is connected to the Internet and thus to the World Wide Web. A server is specialized software on a computer that can receive requests (for information) from other computers (called clients) and answer those requests. A client computer is connected to the World Wide Web by either a direct connection or a modem. As you know by now, the client computer is running a piece of software called a Web browser that translates the electronic signals from the web into text, graphics, sounds, movies, and so on. Web servers answer requests from client computers running browser software. Web servers can serve HTML documents and execute other programs (like CGI files) upon request, using a protocol named Hypertext Transfer Protocol (HTTP).

It is relevant to note that a modem connection to the WWW is much slower than a direct connection. Just as more water can travel through a larger pipe in a set amount of time, so can more information pass through a direct connection than through a modem in a set amount of time.

A special type of server for the web is named an application server. Application servers differ from plain web servers in that they can connect to many other resources outside the web environment. Application servers offer an integrated Web development platform that allows you to connect and manage a variety of enterprise resources such as Web servers, databases, and legacy application systems.

Many companies exist that provide Web site hosting services. In many, if not most, cases it can be far less expensive to contract with one of these services for your hosting needs. The hosting provider is responsible for maintaining the server, any application modules, related services (email, database, etc.) and the network connection. Hosting services often offer a suite of plans to suit your needs. Some hosting services are free and well suited for individual users or organizations. It is

G. O'Toole, *Sustainable Web Ecosystem Design*,
SpringerBriefs in Computer Science, DOI: 10.1007/978-1-4614-7714-3_14,
© The Author(s) 2013

often well worth your time to do a bit of research to identify a Web hosting service that will both meet your current site needs and be able to grow as your site grows. Be sure to select a provider with a good track record for applying server and security patches.

Many popular web servers run on the Unix platform. However, there are web servers for Linux, Windows, and the Macintosh platforms as well. The pros and cons of different web servers and different delivery platforms are beyond the scope of this book. Two of the more common servers are Apache and IIS. Apache is a powerful and free Web server. Apache is so popular, in fact, that it may be the most popular web server currently in use. It began on Unix, but was ported to other platforms. IIS, which stands for Internet Information Server, is a free server from Microsoft. It runs on Windows platforms.

The following recommendations begin to become more technical and deal directly with the server. You may or may not have control over this area if you choose to have someone host your site, but these are questions that you can possibly ask whoever is in charge of administering the server.

If you are developing a web site and you are about to place your site online with a host, you should take in consideration how the potential server provided by the host is connected to the Internet. Are they connected via dial-up modems, DSL, T1 line, T3 line etc? The larger the pipe connecting your host to the Internet, the better performance you will typically see.

One says typically, only because problems can still occur. The server may require faster disk drives and additional processors. If a large pipe is providing a large number of hits, the server must respond just as fast or else a bottleneck will take place. As large numbers of hits are made on the server an added strain is put on the disk drive's ability to seek the requested web pages and transfer the data. To help alleviate this condition, adding more RAM should improve the performance since the CPU will process what is in memory faster than it can retrieve it from a disk. As always, these are not rules but guidelines. Learn about the particular server and its software before making these changes.

Servers also have software upgrades and patches that can dramatically improve performance. Be sure to stay in tune with your operating system vendors updates and install them in the proper order. Be sure to select a hosting service that has a good track record of applying server performance and security patches when they are released.

These last few recommendations may sound easy and with time, you can learn to maintain and administer a server. However, this is an expensive piece to the overall puzzle. Not only in dollars, but in the hours it takes you to properly configure it. If the option exists to have your web site professionally hosted it may very well be worth it. There are many Web hosting services, and it may be time well invested to research them and select a hosting service that not only meets your site needs but that can enable your site to grow as needed.

You do sacrifice some comforts when going with a host. Knowing you are the only activity on the server and having the ability to upgrade when you feel it is appropriate are both good reasons to maintain your own server. Just be aware that the issues surrounding server administration are quite technical and costly.

14.1 Efficiency

Energy consumption of Web servers is a concern. Although Steve Sounder's Performance Golden Rule shows that "80–90 % of the end-user response time is spent on the front end" (Sounders) as opposed to the Web server's back end tasks when serving up Web content, the server is still an area to watch for energy consumption. As a culture and as individuals we tend to think about the Web as a green medium, a communication format that is environmentally healthy largely because we don't use as much paper. However, as a word of informed warning in his *Net Magazine* article "Save the Planet Through Sustainable Web Design," Dr. Peter Markiewicz observes that "the green medium is not (necessarily so) green".

14.2 Performance

Having a great website is not any good if your site's performance is poor. Even though the content, graphics and layout are outstanding, people may not visit the site because the performance is inadequate. Try and test performance as best you can and be aware of different tweaks you can use to try and improve the site's performance.

Whether you are an information technology manager, developer, Webmaster, or data base administrator, if you are tasked with investigating why your intranet or Internet Web site is performing poorly, it is important to understand the scope of this particular task. Consider this scenario from Markiewicz's article:

> Think about an industrial designer creating automobiles. They design cars that are manufactured and placed on the highways. Along the way, engineers may improve their efficiency. But we don't see auto designers creating Hummers, expecting that the engineers can tweak them to get 100 miles per gallon. It can't be done. Engineers may be able to streamline a design, but *initial decisions by designers most determine the final sustainability of a product*. Physical designers know this, and routinely check their designs at the early stage for sustainability.
>
> The web is no different. Design is where the environmental drag of the Web originates, and where it can be fixed. You don't have to be a coder or a site engineer for your decisions to affect the sustainability of the Internet. Your initial work directly controls how energy-hungry the final page will be. Your choices in layout, imagery, and interactive behavior implicitly determine the toxic downstream effects. (Markiewicz)

Site performance is the manner in which your web site responds to requests by the client. Poor site performance is a condition in which a site responds slowly. An efficient server is a necessary node that must be considered when mapping the anatomy of sustainable Web ecosystem design.

14.3 Lightweight Stability

The situation is this: A potential customer comes to your site by typing in your company's web address and waits... and waits... and waits. Several areas are immediately subject to scrutiny. Is it the Internet or intranet network infrastructure, your server software, your server hardware, the client's PC, or your web site's code?

The scope of this problem can possibly encompass all these areas, but there are places to begin for immediate action, and there are long-term techniques that can also be employed to avoid it. No matter what, when tasked with this challenge of improving site performance or "tuning" it, be prepared to take several steps that may require time and technical resources.

When users report problems with your site you want to encourage them to provide as much information as possible. The type of computer they are using, processor speed and amount of memory, operating system they are using and version, the browser they are using and version, and type of network connection could each lend clues to help you determine the cause of a site performance problem. Users may not be able to provide this information, but if they can it will often be a tremendous help.

At the Client (aka the Web browser) there are several areas that can be checked to improve site performance and they take little effort and little time to do. Not everyone on the Internet who is viewing your site will have the same configurations as your PC. You may have a little more control if you are working within a corporation where you have the ability to standardize how each browser settings are made. Your site's standards should be clearly posted in a technical requirements section. This section is often a link off the home page or included in the 'About Us' or 'Help' page. At very least, users should be advised which browsers they may use and which plug-ins or helpers are required.

Having a faster processor on your PC will allow the browser to display web pages that are stored in memory quicker as it renders the markup language faster on your monitor. An additional component that can improve the performance is with the type of graphics card installed on the client PC. Higher end cards can put a strain on the CPU. Needless to say if you purchase a high-end graphics card, ensure there is more than adequate video RAM on the graphics card. This may provide some gains in performance.

Aside from hardware changes, you can also install software that allows you to surf ahead while viewing a web page. This gives the illusion that you are receiving content much faster but in reality you are not. It also may be retrieving pages that you have no interest in viewing. Once again it is only a temporary fix and not a permanent solution to your performance problem. This underscores the importance of testing your site on a variety of platforms—you cannot assume that your development platform will represent the majority of your users.

The options presented here are easy to implement but will not completely solve your problem. They are often worth giving a try to see if they do make an impact.

Another item to note is what time of day you do your web browsing. If you live on the east coast of the United States and get on the Internet first thing in the morning you will notice performance is somewhat better. The thing to remember is that the west coast, for the most part, is still sleeping and not online actively surfing the Internet yet. As the day progresses, not only are your east coast co-workers on the web during their lunch hour, but now the west coast is coming to work and "logging on." So now performance begins to degrade.

With either browser, you will have to experiment with these settings changes to see if they improve performance. But it is very important to note that these are hardware improvements and settings on individual PCs. Not everyone on the Internet who is viewing your site will have the same configurations as your PC. You may have a little more control if you are working within a corporation where you have the ability to standardize how each browser settings are made. Also, you can make a list of recommended settings for viewers of your site, but this may discourage people, and you have no guarantee they will follow your advice.

14.4 Reconciling Project and Host

Performance planning is an important way to maintain that your project will work well with your host. This section deals with some questions that should be addressed during your requirements analysis stage when planning your Web project concerning the host and your needed efficiencies.

Before beginning the analysis involved in network component you should consider and understand once again the goal of the Web project. What is the purpose of the project? Will it have peak usage times, will it provide the ability to download or upload large files, will it need to have secure sections, etc.? Knowing this will help one understand the network requirement. Many Web sites have failed, or gained a poor reputation, because they were unable to grow with their user base.

If your web server is connected to the network via modems you may need to make necessary changes to the server to handle user requests differently than handling requests if you were on a faster connection such as a T1 line. This is done with the web server software.

If you have chosen an ISP to host your web site it would be a good idea to explain the goals of the planned web site to them. The host may or may not be able to provide some of the services that a client may request. For example, if a client is a radio station or a multimedia provider of sorts, they may desire to stream their media. Servers require special software for this activity to take place and it typically has a high price. Streaming media will also require a network connection that provides more capacity than a dial up connection. At home, for example, your telephone line may be used for modem connections. Today, higher speeds are commonplace in the home, and other options are usually available at an institution capable of supporting (physically and financially) such high-speed lines. Although the statistics vary, the 2012 estimate is approximately 60 % of US households have broadband Internet connections with plans by the United States Department of Commerce to continue to improve the infrastructure and increase speed and access in the near future.

Initially your client's web site requirements may be limited in scope. They may not understand or envision how the site can potentially grow. If they do not, it becomes your responsibility to at least make them aware that the site may grow. If you are hosting the site yourself and not using a host, this stage becomes very important. The selection of the server hardware and software becomes top priority.

At first you may want to stick with products that are proven and reliable. Be aware if your server is to be shared with other software such as other networking responsibilities or database software. Either of these will probably use processing power that may be needed by the web site.

Ask yourself what tasks will the web site be performing. Will you need a separate server to be your web server? If so, it is recommended that you have several small disks instead of one large disk. Several smaller disks, as seen in a Redundant Array of Inexpensive Devices (RAID) will typically prove to be a better performer than having the server seek data across a large disk.

Be sure to know if your server is scalable. Understand whether or not additional processors, additional drives, or additional RAM can be added easily. This process should not be a major evolution but should be something that requires little effort to complete. One other item to note is that regardless of how fast your server is, it will not do you any good if you have a slow network connection or vice versa.

Whether you are a developer, administrator, or manager it is important to understand the importance of planning. Giving thought to the scope and scalability of the proposed website is a key indicator of a professional. Whichever role you are playing, knowing that site performance can be planned is crucial, but also remember that technology changes rapidly and what might hold fast as a rule with current server or network technology may not hold true one year from now.

14.4.1 Content Considerations

As you design your web site there are things you can do to make your server work easier and produce content quicker. Typically, you can start by keeping your file sizes down. If your visitors come to your site and wait more than 12 s for an HTML file to download then you have a potential problem. If your pages take longer to display than this on your target system and connection speed, it may be wise to begin thinking of using pages that provide summary information so that the visitor knows what they are getting themselves into before downloading it.

Remember a browser parses the information in the file and this requires work by the PC's processor. Having smaller files means less parsing and less work by the CPU. An HTML file can easily be pared down by removing redundant or useless tags. Keeping limited information in comments, if any at all, is one tip. Another tip is to keep information with the tag fairly short.

14.4.2 Image Slices

Several web development tools on the market assist in cleaning up HTML in order to make file sizes smaller. Dreamweaver allows developers to run a wizard that goes through their code and remove unnecessary tags. A great deal of unnecessary code is used when you use some of the popular WYSIWYG tools and/or word processors to create webpages.

Keep graphics included on your webpage in the 10–24 Kb range to ensure quicker downloads. But even this range tends to be large. You can help out the browser and people who turn off images by using the ALT tag to describe your graphic. Also, use the height and width parameter for sizing your graphic. This frees the browser from examining the graphic to determine the proper size.

Try slicing the image into smaller files or removing colors from the graphic to decrease the file size. Also remember that certain graphic formats compress better than others. In general, vector graphics have a smaller file size than JPEGs and GIFs.

14.4.3 Measuring Performance

It is easy to say a site is performing poorly if it takes a considerable amount of time to download content, but there are also techniques and software that measure this performance quantitatively. Performance is often measured through the use of benchmarks. Benchmarks allow us to generate statistics about the level of performance under a set condition and then make a comparison to a set of data in order to determine the level of:

- *Efficiency* is a mathematical formula stating throughput divided by utilization,
- *Latency* is the amount of time it takes to see a downloaded file begin after the time it was actually requested,
- *Throughput* is a term that can be used interchangeably with *bandwidth*. It can be thought of as the number of bits transmitted,
- *Utilization* refers to the percentage of usage for a given component. This component can be network bandwidth, a storage disk, memory, etc.

These four parameters can all be measured to varying degrees.

Many tests exist but before doing so you need to ensure whatever test you set up mimics the actual environment during operation. In other words, find a test that will actually mimic what you will be doing in the real world. If all your users are going to be connecting via 56.6 Kb Modems then the test should be run as if several users are connecting to your web site at that speed.

There are many vendors on the market today that provide benchmarks and services to measure them. Some vendors simulate what it would be like if you have several hundred visitors making requests to your WebServer and monitor the results. Other vendors allow you to set your variables for running the test and provide an extensive list of options that make the test more applied, or real world, than theoretical.

As a final point, remember that benchmark tests are only valuable if you can mimic very closely what it will be like when your site is online and accessible. xxx is a necessary node that must be considered when mapping the anatomy of sustainable Web ecosystem design.

14.5 Security

The security available for users of TCP/IP networks, like the Internet and the World Wide Web, has become critical for organizations', businesses', and individuals' data, information, and knowledge. This topic will provide an overview of the basic security concepts including authentication, authorization, non-repudiation, and data integrity that must be kept in mind when considering your project as part of a sustainable Web ecosystem. It will outline and describe the major types of security including physical, social, host, network, application security.

Imagine the following scenario: Someone comes to your home while you're sleeping or even while you're working around your yard. Carefully using an open window, the intruder creeps into your living room and begins examining all of your things. He picks up first one item, then another, looking over each one to see if he'd like to keep it. After going quietly through your entire house without your noticing, he sets the catch on the window so he can return later, when you're not home or when you simply aren't watching. It will be then that he will take all of what he wants. How would you feel, upon noticing that your things had been slightly moved? What would your feeling be if you returned later from a store and found all of your property gone?

When people are robbed, they understandably feel both angry and violated. This scenario, however, also describes what happens when a computer is attacked. A hacker who finds vulnerability in your system can come in, look around, and even leave herself an opening so she can return and hijack your property at leisure. Security of your computer, therefore, is important. This lesson serves as an overview of general issues involving computer security.

People unfamiliar with security issues tend to see security as a nuisance. They may believe the measures needed to provide security are not necessary or cost prohibitive, or that they obstruct the user's experience. However, in an environment like the World Wide Web where anonymity is so easy to achieve, security is essential. As a site designer/developer, you have a responsibility to protect the security of user information. You also have a responsibility to encourage your users to be aware of any security issues when they share information online. Four key security concepts are presented here:

1. Authentication—Authentication is one of the most basic security concepts and is very important. Authentication is proving that you are who you say you are. Proof of identity can be accomplished through:

   • A shared secret (i.e. password)
   • Something you have (i.e. smart card, certificates, etc.)
   • Something you are (i.e. retinal scans, thumb prints, etc.)
     Some of these authentication options may sound futuristic, but all are a reality. For example, most of you probably use a password every day of your lives. This password could be one to your computer at work, one to your favorite Web site, or even the pin number for your ATM card or calling card.

2. Authorization—As a Webmaster or security specialist, once you have proven a person is who he or she claims to be, you must determine what this user is allowed to do. For example, when you use your ATM card, you are only allowed to make transactions for accounts that are in your name. This theory applies to the computer world. For example, just as you would not want strangers to have access to your personal bank account, you would not want every user on your local area network to have full access to your machine. Authorization is managed by assigning users to groups having a specific set of rights, or by assigning a set of rights to each user.

3. Non-Repudiation—This is a legal term that means evidence is necessary to prove that a person who claims authorship of an act actually performed the act.

4. Data Integrity—As used here, integrity refers to the data sent between two hosts. It simply means that the data sent is exactly the same as the data received.

14.5.1 Types of Security

Maintaining a secure computing environment is an ongoing process that requires attention to detail, and all five types together are necessary for a truly secure environment. Although we have separated each of the five types of security for the purposes of our discussion, in reality, each type is intricately interrelated and interdependent upon the others.

1. Physical—Physical security is typically one of the most overlooked components in the security chain. To achieve physical security, you must consider

who has physical access to your machine and what that person(s) can physically do. Can he steal the machine or extract important information?

2. Social—Social security is probably the most difficult component to achieve because it involves users, not computers. Social security requires training your users in good computing practices, including creating good passwords, changing passwords frequently, not giving out information via e-mail or the phone, and so on.

3. Host—Host security is the security of local computing resources. These resources can include file systems, local accounts, exported file systems (called file shares), printers attached to the system, patching, or updating of the operating system, and so on. Host security is usually in the hands of the individuals responsible for the daily maintenance of your hardware and software systems. These people must be trained on host security issues and have processes in place to ensure host security is always considered. Some measures taken to secure the host may seem obtrusive to your users, and they may complain of inconvenience when you try to implement measures.

4. Network—Network security is the security of the resources that handle your data while in transit from one host to another. This is quite an exciting and interesting field, because it is so multidimensional. Network security not only involves securing your data, but also involves securing all the hardware that is used to get your data from one place to another. Often a firewall, a device for blocking unwanted traffic, will be used.

5. Application—Application security is dependent on all of the other security components in a system. Application security encompasses everything related to and involved in the writing of an application—including:

- good code in the application itself
- the browser that delivers it (in the case of Web-based applications)
- the database that stores any information collected
- how data is transmitted over the network.

14.5.2 Web Security

Web security begins with the design and development of secure sites. This section will list a few areas where Web site security can be improved.

14.5.3 Site Design

A safe Web experience begins with the design of a site, specifically with user interactions. Are you requiring or requesting that users provide private information (such as an email address or telephone number)? Many users will naively provide that information, unaware of the potential for it to be compromised and used against them in identity theft. Sites should be designed such that you are only gathering the information needed to provide the user with the requested service or information.

Will your site contain company information that should be secure? Assessing the security risk for all information stored by the Web site (and its back-end DBMS) will guide you on applying controls. However, availability is also a component in security—do you have adequate backup strategies to ensure that critical information is available to those who will need it in event of a site compromise or failure?

The specifications for Web site design should include a security risk assessment to ensure that your clients are aware of potential risks. Cookies should be used that do not allow for tracking by other sites. Integrity suggests that users should be made aware of all information gathered about them—even if the purpose is only to develop metrics for site improvement. If you cannot justify their use, do not use cookies.

14.5.4 Site Development

If the site contains scripts for dynamic content, or uses a DBMS back-end, then special care must be taken to avoid SQL-injection attacks on the site or the use of script injection to compromise user data. These attacks (accounting for over 50 % of all Web vulnerabilities) can be easily avoided through appropriate coding practices. If you are outsourcing script development be sure you contract with a company that has a track record of secure coding. Server and site deployment should be documented in a way to ensure that testing is conducted effectively and that upgrades do not open new vulnerabilities. Utilize secure HTTP connections for transfer of all user data. Encrypt sensitive user data such as credit-card numbers and other personally-identifiable information.

14.5.5 Site Management

Server administrators should ensure that security upgrades for system components are applied as soon as they are released. If you contract with a Web hosting service be sure that they have a good track record in security. If you administer the servers yourself you may want to contract with a penetration testing service to ensure that your servers and components have the most current security patches applied. Your site should have a User Agreement that specifies the user information gathered and maintained and the conditions under which it may be shared with business partners.

14.5.6 User Considerations

Users should always be sure that their Operating System and Browser have the latest security upgrades applied. Users should obtain, install, keep current, and periodically run good anti-malware and anti-spyware software. Users should be careful browsing the Web from an account that has administrator privileges. This allows malware to install itself on the user's computer without their notification. Many of the worst instances of malware (such as rootkits) operate this way. Users should always create a user account, in addition to the administrator account, and ensure that it does not have administrator privileges. They should then only use the user account when browsing the Web. If a program requires administrator privileges, such as when the user is intentionally installing a new program or upgrade, a window will open to ask for permission. Use of a user account (the least-privilege account) is claimed by Microsoft to stop over 65 % of all malware infections. Users may want to utilize one of a number of free services that alert them when they are attempting to link to a Web site that has a poor reputation. Google Chrome has built-in security measures that will warn a user when they are attempting to access a Web site with potential risks.

Finally, users should beware of Social Engineering tactics that attempt to trick them into voluntarily revealing personal information. Examples abound, such as emails claiming to be from a foreign banker and promising to transfer a large sum of money into the user's bank account—but requiring the account numbers to proceed. Another example is an email or Web page promising to provide free information or software—when the user selects the hyperlink malware is downloaded to the user's computer in the background. If a deal seems to be too good to be true it probably is. Also Web users need to be aware of providing too much information on social networking sites. For example, posting pictures from your family summer vacation at the shore could alert a thief that your home is unattended. Better to wait until you get home and then post the pictures.

Suggested Web Resource(s):

W3C Web Security: http://www.w3.org/Security

Chapter 15
Post Launch

Just because you have version one of your project created, secured safely on a trusted host, and performing flawlessly, don't think your work is done. Often times post launch, or the continuing maintenance, updating, and upgrading of your project is a necessary node that must be considered when mapping the anatomy of sustainable Web ecosystem design.

15.1 Maintenance

Maintenance of a Web project can come in many forms. From periodic security patch installations to adding, editing, or deleting people in a directory, there is always work to be done on most Web-based projects. The key here is to do the work. You don't want your project running stale and outdated content. You want your data to stay relevant to the aims of the project. You don't want to keep people in a directory who have left an organization and may still be able to log into the site, for example. Some Web sites for example maintain mirror versions for development and testing sites. These all need to be maintained and kept current. These are all part of the maintenance of a live project on the Web. For sure, your individual circumstances will warrant other tasks on your list.

15.2 Workflow

If you are running a Web site, for example, on a content management system, the workflow settings will empower your content providers and free you up as the Web manager to do other things. Workflow allows certain users in groups or as individuals to be assigned permissions to carry out certain tasks on the Web site, and not be able to carry out certain other tasks on the site. So, for example, you may have a group of content providers, writers and image specialists who create

G. O'Toole, *Sustainable Web Ecosystem Design*,
SpringerBriefs in Computer Science, DOI: 10.1007/978-1-4614-7714-3_15,

new news and events objects for a site, but they don't have the rights to publish this new content, to make it live on the site. Your content managers are the people who will approve and publish. This is a simple workflow scenario. Setting up an efficient workflow for your project will make this part of the post launch maintenance efficient during the life span of the project.

15.3 Content Provider Groups, (e)Teaching, (e)Learning

Content provider or user groups are extremely useful as a stable resource to train, ask and answer questions, and generally keep open the lines of communication about the processes the providers are using in order to do what they needed to do in their jobs every day. Conversation at content provider group meetings can quickly evolve into informative discussion about help, best practice, and standardizing practices for your organization and the Web in general for your content providers. This type of group can be helpful to designers and developers, as well as content managers and providers of all levels. If you are running a content managed site providing your content providers with the direction they need is a necessary node that must be considered when mapping the anatomy of sustainable Web ecosystem design.

It is smart to include all Web-related workers as needed within your organization in your group in order to create the most productive environment. If not everyone can make your meetings, or you have too big of a group to be efficient in a working meeting setting, it is helpful to create smaller, sub-groups, or at the very least, make the meetings available to attend remotely, and record and archive the meeting in video and written minutes formats. This is useful in creating an archive or the groups' progress, and also makes the meeting content and any helpful resolutions easily available on the organization's intranet. To make this a seamless process, create a home site for the group within the intranet of your organization. That way all users have proper access, while the whole world won't have the ability to look in on what you are doing.

In the past I have created highly successful content provider groups and helped others create their own. In one instance, at the Social Science Research Institute at Penn State University we formed a group and thereafter kept a helpful group Web site updated with instructional notes for users of the group to learn about the new features of the site. The site includes modules for upcoming meetings, past meetings with notes, Web support information for the Institute, an outline of what the groups goals are, encouragement and direction on how users can generate fruitful discussions and ask questions through comments, and other Web related help materials. All of this is available to the group members easily and conveniently within their organization's intranet from a short, memorable URL (Fig. 15.1).

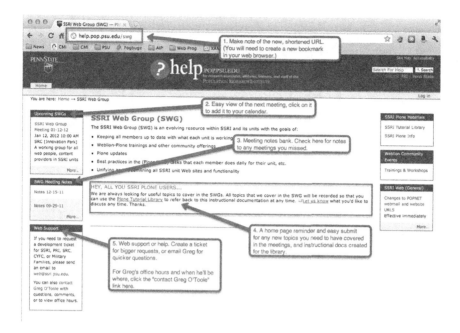

Fig. 15.1 The home screen of a Web content provider group at the Social Science Research Institute at Penn State University with instructional notes for users of the group to learn about the new features of the site. The site includes modules for upcoming meetings, past meetings with notes, Web support information for the Institute, an outline of what the groups goals are, encouragement and direction on how users can generate fruitful discussions and ask questions through comments, and other Web related help materials. All of this is available to the group members easily and conveniently within their organization's intranet from a short, memorable URL

15.4 User Groups, Community

Look for communities that have sprung up around the technologies your or your organization is using for whatever type of Web work you are doing. Some groups have regular, resident meetings, some have virtual meetings, some include a hybrid, and some have no meetings at all, but share a common online chat room, for example, and communicate via internet relay chat. However your groups meet and exchange problems and solutions, sharing ideas and solutions is a necessary node that must be considered when mapping the anatomy of sustainable Web ecosystem design (Fig. 15.2).

Fig. 15.2 The home screen of the State College, Pennsylvania Plone Users Group (http://www.meetup.com/Plone-Users-Group). The site is a convenient way to share everything useful that the user group creates or works on. The site includes easy to install ics files with relevant information for each of the meeting events, news, member profiles, and a keyword map that describes the group's interests

15.5 Analytics

Web analytics means knowing your users. Perhaps the obvious first choice here is Google Analytics. It is free, effective, and powerful. But to be sure there are many options when it comes to tracking user behavior on your site as it relates to pages accessed, new visits, return visits, Web browsers used, operating systems of your users, countries of origin, search engine of origin, key words used to find your site, and many more. Analytics can be a powerful statistical tool to gauge not only user demographics, but user behavior as well (Fig. 15.3).

You can find out which parts of your site your users are most frequently visiting and then make those areas more prominent in your navigation, for example. In another scenario, as a designer, it is important for you to have a sense of where the browser market is headed. This helps in making decisions regarding how to design and what features to support for the end-user audience. This can be accomplished by collecting statistics on the server that is running your Web site. These statistics can provide insight on the type of browser and version that are most typically viewing your site. By analyzing these statistics, you can adjust your design efforts toward the audience that you are serving.

There is a whole industry based on user analytics and what can be done with it to optimize your Web project, promote your goods or services, and understand your users. Analytics certainly are a node of sustainable Web ecosystem design.

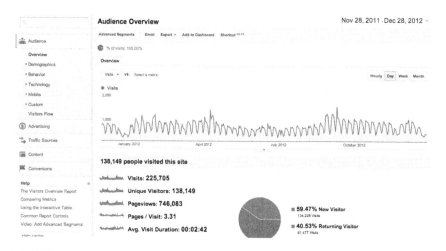

Fig. 15.3 A quick Google Analytics view of one year of http://ist.psu.edu. Google Analytics is only one software solution for tracking Web user statistics in terms of demographics, behavior, technology, mobility, ad use, traffic sources, and much more

Suggested Web Resource(s):

Google Analytics: http://www.google.com/analytics
Yahoo Web Analytics: http://web.analytics.yahoo.com
Web Analytics on Wikipedia: http://en.wikipedia.org/wiki/Web_analytics
Piwik Real Time Analytics: http://piwik.org

Chapter 16
Education

Harold Adams Innis (1894–1952) knew that the university as a culturally beneficial and intellectually necessary environment was not perfect, in fact, far from it. He devoted much of his life to establishing and improving the higher education system of Canada. Among Innis' many contributions is the clarification that borrowing from the past cultural milieu toward the new must be a rather selective process in order to avoid an over abundance of unneeded cultural baggage which simultaneously leaves a conditional void or a type of intellectual incompleteness. This progressive absence is necessary so that there is always a culturally perceived need for new ideas, and so that there is room for these innovative ideas to enter and flourish. Without this necessary incompleteness, the sense of a need for new ideas and innovation is aborted. Innis came to the conclusion that it is an effect of modern mediated communication, with its ever-increasing attribute of flawless efficiency and quantity of content (the record of cultural baggage), that rather senselessly and somewhat automatically fills this void and, in a sense, renders the incomplete complete, but in an insignificant way. For Innis this was a great crisis for the West, and a sign of its eventual downfall.

As far back as the early part of the second half of the twentieth century it was certainly not such common sentiment that human consumption has risen to the point that this activity alone is effectively altering the Earth's atmosphere. Perhaps the rather esoteric Club of Rome Dossiers (1965–1984) would have helped to enlighten more people on the idea that "the world system is simply not ample enough, nor generous enough to accommodate much longer such egocentric and conflictive behavior by its inhabitants." In its 1972 paper the Executive Committee of the Club of Rome warns in it's *Commentary to the Limits to Growth* that "the closer we come to the material limits to the planet, the more difficult this problem will be to tackle" ("Club of Rome "The Dossiers" 1965–1984"). However, the culture of mass consumption has done exactly this. The economic system, over many years, has changed the composition of the planet's atmosphere, buying has affected the way the Earth functions. We've extracted, moved, burned, shipped, and consumed fossil fuels to an alarming degree, raising the percentage of carbon in the atmosphere. For starters, this has a direct effect on the weather around the

G. O'Toole, *Sustainable Web Ecosystem Design*,
SpringerBriefs in Computer Science, DOI: 10.1007/978-1-4614-7714-3_16,
© The Author(s) 2013

world. Adding carbon changes the weather, this process alters the ways people see and experience the world around them first hand. The world around the consumer is a system, or a series of systems interlinked. It is in a similar manner that the amount of information that we've produced, consumed, processed at increasing rates of bits and bytes per second, that we have effectively altered our sense of reality: the ways in which we see ourselves playing apart in the world around us. Like adding an overabundance of carbon atoms into the atmosphere fundamentally changes that environment, introducing a profusion of information in the form of messages makes cardinal edits to human psychology. In this case the system that our human behavior has altered is not the Earth's atmosphere, but is the sense of what we refer to as reality. Reality has been changed by the messages of mass media and the information they contain. It is our obligation to live with these messages surrounding us every day.

The human being is engulfed by narrative. In the mass media (i.e. Internet) world, it is arguably true that most of what people discuss and concern themselves with on a daily basis is known from their surrounding narrative. At the very least, there is much more narrative knowledge to sift through with the advent of the various static, mobile, dynamic, syndicated communication technologies, not to mention the force of the active audience.

Everything is information. The good news is that in the current information age people have convenient, fingertip access to continual, global content. The bad news is that in the current information age people have this same convenient, fingertip access to continual, global content. At first the free flow of information seems convenient, empowering, and endlessly beneficial for those world citizens with access to it. Industry takes great pains to bridge the social agency and access digital divides. Companies are continuously inventing and marketing smaller pocket-sized devices with which can communicate instantaneously and in a variety of ways. Contemporary culture spends vast amounts of money every day for more connections, faster networks, and ubiquitous wifi. There is a current industry determined pseudo-narrative in place claiming that all of this informational access can only be a good thing. Upon a closer look, one has to wonder if more content can ever be too much content.

Historically, information production and distribution has always equaled a certain amount of power for those in control of these processes. In the one-to-many relationship of mass media producers control what the inactive viewers see, hear, and read. It has been shown that through the event of broadcast, news outlets have had the power to shape the relative importance a viewer may apply to certain content. This process can even influence which issues are thought to be most serious and most important to the viewing public. This historic imbalance between the agencies of media producers and those of media consumers is changing as a result of the available media communication technology, creating a new type of media consumer: the active viewer. As a result of this influx, as media consumers in the Internet age, populations and the individual are in need of a critical regiment to control and understand what they choose to digest as part of a media diet. Through experience it is known that too much of anything is not a good thing.

As with the over-consumption of sugar, fat, cholesterol, and salt for the human body, today, as media consumers, individuals have the responsibility of their media diets and in dealing with the potential for an easy, cheap, convenient diet of fast food, always with an eye of awareness toward information glut.

Further, there is a media outlet available for nearly every point of view that exists. Certainly with a single Google search, for example, a blog entry or forum post, no matter how well or otherwise written and no matter the language, can be located on just about any topic, including posts that fall on both sides (or any side) of any story. However, how does the information consumer know where to find the facts that the news media are supposed to transparently provide in order that users become and remain informed, knowledgeable citizens? Where is the objectification that the media is supposed to promote in order that viewers and readers make informed decisions on their own or within their local critical social circles? There is any number of bloggers out there, but which one is correct, if any? CNN, the BBC, and Der Spiegel run their content distribution twenty-four hours a day, but is what they are pouring into millions of living rooms, computers, cell phones really important for the average citizen to know? If not all of it, how much of it? Today, in the Internet age, these are the questions that can only be answered by each individual as a living member of planet Earth. Gone are the days of the "good" informed citizen needing only to subscribe and read the local newspaper each morning, and the evening edition at night. In the current information epoch users have many more decisions to make, and the power to make the right ones. With a little thoughtfulness and effort, users can do this to the benefit of themselves and their communities. The bad news is that in the information age there is continual, global information content at the user's fingertips. The good news is that in the information age there is continual, global content available at the user's fingertips.

In the contemporary media-rich world, there is now, more than ever, the need for an applicable theoretical and quantitative investigation on these questions which involve the ideas of working academics, writers whose work on the nature of media, power, information, human psychology, and mass movements contribute to an advanced academic foundation in media theory and can help viewers to understand the effects of the prevailing condition of the world today.

The present social, economic, political, and cultural conditions, as they are, certainly are difficult to effectively navigate. In the postmodern, as individuals in a larger community, media consumers can no longer rely on the grand narratives they once could to show them the way. When the nuclear family has broken up, where do young people turn for guidance? When the religions cause wars and endless controversy where do we turn for spiritual guidance? When community leaders, politicians, and industry CEOs spend more time defending themselves from fraudulent charges and prison sentences who can we trust? When a daily avalanche of consumerist messages point viewers toward consumption as the way to happiness from where do people find the strength to resist if they chose to do so? How do they even know that they can?

Sut Jhally very clearly points out "today's hyper-consumerism is driven by ever more sophisticated advertising and public relations techniques. The specific product is secondary. What they're really selling is lifestyle (and) ideology." It is essential for viewers in these investigations to look at the wide potential for acceptance of the messages of mass media texts. It is equally important to inquire into how, as a culture, users have the potential, consciously or otherwise, to allow these mediated messages to actually, in many ways, become at least part of the significance of the daily existence, and to keep in mind that ultimately it is the individual citizen who needs to remain in control of the information they access, how they react to it, and what they consider to be significant and true. One might warn the audience member to do their best to think critically on every topic they consider and do their best not to be swayed in any way by beautiful actors, big budgets, slick graphics, or political agendas: a task that is much easier said than done to be sure.

These reasons only scratch the surface as to why media education is so important, probably more so today than ever. The constant and pressing messages emphasizing the self, image, and self-image, the rhetoric of politics, and the desires imagined by an economics that fosters created wants all speak to the need for media education. The identity construction of every individual and group counts on it. Media education not only needs to be primary in every educational system, but needs to start at the elementary school level. Most beneficially, media education needs to start at home as soon as any child reaches the age where they are old enough to find interest in their first book or cartoon. This is something that everyone can agree upon. Let us become more aware. Education is a necessary node that must be considered when mapping the anatomy of sustainable Web ecosystem design.

Chapter 17
Policy

Policies around the Web are an important part of the keeping the Web ecosystem sustainable. It is an evolving node of the anatomy. The first 20 years or so of the popular use of the Internet were referred to as the wild west of the Web. This, for the most part, is true. Without a lot of regulating standards around such issues as who can use the Web, how it can be used, and who or what controls these patterns of use, etc. the Web has evolved largely in an unregulated way. In many ways this is beneficial for issues such as free speech and freedom of access and use, especially for good reasons. At the same time, there is not as much protection from inappropriate content for children and teens, for example. So, as you can see there are two sides to this coin. Because this condition won't last forever in this wild west state, we need to be aware of the issues being discussed, who is involved, what their positions are and why. Is it good for a large corporation to regulate and tier Internet use, for example? Why or why not? In a lot of ways, the idea of being an informed consumer or citizen harkens back to the early days of the newspaper. We understand that being a member of a democracy obligates us to stay abreast of the many issues alive today, and to know a little something about the key players and their motives. This is the only way to stay involved in a democracy and to play a positive role in that social organization. The Web issues that can turn into policies and maybe even laws are important for use to be familiar with in that they have at least the potential to influence our lives, our work, and perhaps even the lives and liberties of our children and grandchildren. Some of the important Web issues of today are discussed in this section. It is important to be familiar with these issues as contributors of a sustainable Web ecosystem.

The Electronic Frontier Foundation

It is important to bring up the work of groups such as the Electronic Frontier Foundation (EFF) when discussing the impact and relevance of social issues related to the Web. Understanding the magnitude and role of the Internet as far back as 1990, the EFF has been at the forefront of addressing and pursuing legal action around free speech, fair use, privacy, innovation, international, and transparency in the context of the Web.

G. O'Toole, *Sustainable Web Ecosystem Design*,
SpringerBriefs in Computer Science, DOI: 10.1007/978-1-4614-7714-3_17,
© The Author(s) 2013

From the Internet to the iPod, technologies are transforming our society and empowering us as speakers, citizens, creators, and consumers. When our freedoms in the networked world come under attack, the Electronic Frontier Foundation (EFF) is the first line of defense. EFF broke new ground when it was founded in 1990—well before the Internet was on most people's radar—and continues to confront cutting-edge issues defending free speech, privacy, innovation, and consumer rights today. From the beginning, EFF has championed the public interest in every critical battle affecting digital rights.

Blending the expertise of lawyers, policy analysts, activists, and technologists, EFF achieves significant victories on behalf of consumers and the general public. EFF fights for freedom primarily in the courts, bringing and defending lawsuits even when that means taking on the US government or large corporations. By mobilizing more than 140,000 concerned citizens through our Action Center, EFF beats back bad legislation. In addition to advising policymakers, EFF educates the press and public.

EFF is a donor-funded nonprofit and depends on your support to continue successfully defending your digital rights. Litigation is particularly expensive; because two-thirds of our budget comes from individual donors, every contribution is critical to helping EFF fight—and win—more cases (EFF).

Visit the Electronic Frontier Foundation on the Web to learn about the legal details of many of their cases, get educated on the big issues they are tackling, get current with updated news, and sign petitions and take other action as a concerned citizen of a democracy that can flourish with the sustainable Web ecosystem.

Suggested Web Resource(s):

Electronic Frontier Foundation: http://www.eff.org.

17.1 Web Standards: The W3C

In the software industry, there are often times initiatives to develop standards, or protocols, that similar pieces of software use. The World Wide Web Consortium (W3C) was founded in September 1994, and is responsible for setting the standards for HTML, and for deciding what is "official" HTML and what is not.

Browser companies frequently release HTML tags that are not official HTML tags as defined by W3C. These browser-specific HTML tags are dubbed HTML extensions. The mission of the W3C is: "promoting interoperability and encouraging an open forum for discussion," thus helping to standardize HTML. The Consortium is where companies and organizations to which the future of the Web is important come to discuss and agree on new common computer protocols.

Suggested Web Resource(s):

W3C Web Standards: http://www.w3.org/standards.

17.2 Freedom of Speech/Human Rights

It has been observed that today the Internet is doing for the Middle East what Johannes Gutenberg's printing press with moveable type did for Christianity's Protestant Reformation in the fifteenth century. That is, a new media communication technology is allowing for the dissemination of new ideas to spread among the population, and no longer be relegated to a select few. The technology creates a context in which there are limited barriers to the transference of information among the people. This technology creates a condition where the power structure that has been in place is no longer as strong nor as influential as it once was specifically or in part due to the abilities of the people, those lower in the power hierarchy, to have new ideas, share new ideas, and circumvent the old structures. This was witnessed in the rise of the Protestant Reformation where the high numbers of inexpensively printed Bibles, along with sharing these Bibles among the people across Europe altered the strict, powerful hierarchy of the Catholic Church. When individuals are empowered, the need for powerful leaders is diminished. Similarly since around 2009 the use of mobile technology and social media among the people of the Middle East has played an important role in the political and social changes that have taken place.

The challenge here is that the Web needs to remain open for freedom of speech every way, but at the same time the Web also needs to offer proper protection for children and youth from cyber bullying, pornography, and other negative influences.

Suggested Web Resource(s):

W3C Web Standards: http://www.w3.org/standards
Electronic Frontier Foundation: http://www.eff.org
Freedom Forum: http://www.freedomforum.org
The Victims of Iranian Censorship (VOICE) Act on Wikipedia:
http://en.wikipedia.org/wiki/Victims_of_Iranian_Censorship_Act
Brookings Institute Research on U.S. Foreign Policy on Internet Freedom:
http://www.brookings.edu/research/reports/2012/10/25-ediplomacy-hanson-internet-freedom

17.3 Politics

To be sure, there is clearly some overlap here with the freedom of speech issue, however, it is important enough to discuss this as a separate issues as well. The Web needs to (continue to) be an effective tool for government and the people, and at the same time the Web needs to be policed for the abuse of power and political terrorism. This is certainly not an easy balance to strike. Here we are mostly concerned with the ways in which governments perform their daily activities in managing their work, addressing issues, balancing budgets, spending tax dollars, and all of the while, keeping the public informed of what they are doing because in a democracy that is the right of the people.

Suggested Web Resource(s):

W3C Web Standards: http://www.w3.org/standards
Electronic Frontier Foundation: http://www.eff.org
U.S. Obama Open Government Initiative: http://www.whitehouse.gov/open
U.S. President Obama's Transparency of Plans: http://www.barackobama.com/issues
Obama's Transparency Statement:
http://www.whitehouse.gov/the_press_office/TransparencyandOpenGovernment.

17.4 Health

As with the social and political changes that evolve with the advent of a technology such as the Web, we need to be aware of the health-related changes that can come about medically, physiologically, mentally, and emotionally for individuals and society.

Suggested Web Resource(s):

Pew Internet and the American Life Project: http://pewinternet.org
Electronic Frontier Foundation: http://www.eff.org

17.5 Economics

The Web must be maintained in a way that optimizes potential opportunities for businesses large and small to be productive. The balance here is that the Web also needs to be safe from identity theft and other financial fraud so that ecommerce can continue to grow.

Suggested Web Resource(s):

Business USA: http://business.usa.gov
National Cyber Security Alliance: http://www.staysafeonline.org/business-safe-online
Electronic Frontier Foundation: http://www.eff.org

17.6 Open Accessibility

As has been eluded to many times in this book, the bottom line is that now and forever moving forward, the Web and any new media communication technologies that come along and become available to us, all need to be freely, equally accessible to all users. This includes Web users on this side of the social digital divide, that is to say, those people who want to use the Web. This also includes Web users on this side of the access digital divide. The access digital divide is the distance between the places in the world where Internet access is available and those where it is not. The areas of the world where Web access isn't available become smaller every day. Soon there will be no access digital divide. And, of course, the Web needs to remain equally available to users with disabilities as well.

In October 2011, the *Washington Post* reported U.S. Secretary of State Hillary Clinton's Senior Adviser for Innovation, Alec Ross, as saying:

> If the great struggles of the twentieth century were between left and right, the conflict of the twenty-first century will be between open and closed. The President and the Secretary of State have made it clear where they stand on this: for openness, with an open Internet at its core.

Suggested Web Resource(s):

W3C Web Standards: http://www.w3.org/standards
Brookings Institute Research on U.S. Foreign Policy on Internet Freedom: http://www.brookings.edu/research/reports/2012/10/25-ediplomacy-hanson-internet-freedom

17.7 Environment

The Web needs to be environmentally safe and conservative. Earlier in this book the energy consumption of Web servers was touched on. This also includes bandwidth considerations and efficiencies, as well as carbon footprints on the plants and factories that make the hardware that we use on a daily basis. Environmental impact is all around us every day, just like the Web. Sustainability concerns need to be reconciled between the two.

Suggested Web Resource(s):

Steve Sounders' Performance Golden Rule (resources):
http://www.stevesouders.com/blog/2012/02/10/the-performance-golden-rule

Pete Markiewicz's Net Magazine article on sustainable Web design (resources):
http://www.netmagazine.com/features/save-planet-through-sustainable-web-
design
Electronic Frontier Foundation: http://www.eff.org

17.8 Education

There is no question of the changes that the Web is bringing to the 500+ year old
education model that humans have become accustomed to. Today the most revered
universities on the planet are taking part or leading the way in offering online
degrees, or going further creating free, open courses online. Education as become
omnipresent including modes of teaching, learning, and collaborating on research.
Where this new, changing educational model will lead we can only guess, but it is
certainly up to us to mold it and shape it into a fair, open model so that education
can be available to all people in all parts of the world who want it.

Suggested Web Resource(s):

Coursera: http://www.coursera.org
OpenClass: http://www.openclass.com
EdEx by Harvard, MIT, Berkeley, and Others: https://www.edx.org
Open Yale: http://oyc.yale.edu
MIT OpenCourseware: http://ocw.mit.edu
Lynda.com: http://www.lynda.com (http://lynda.psu.edu)

Chapter 18
Philosophy of Technology

Great minds have been considering technology since far before Socrates and Plato argued over the advent of the written word. To collect all of these ideas into one publication would be quite an ambitious feat. However, in this section we can take very brief bits of influence from some of the media and technology philosophers who have made a significant contribution to their fields and consider them in our context of the sustainable Web ecosystem. Certainly this is neither an exhaustive list of relevant philosophers nor the ideas toward the study and understanding of the impact of a sustainable Web ecosystem, but this section is a very basic introduction to some of the ideas. This section can be used as a springboard of sorts to further study around the ideas of media theory and the philosophy of technology. At any rate, an open mind to some of these ideas is a necessary node that must be considered when mapping the anatomy of sustainable Web ecosystem design.

18.1 Fredrick Jameson

One characteristic mark of contemporary, or postmodern, times is a declination of what philosophers such as Fredrick Jameson call the metanarrative, that is, the big picture by which we structure the observations and assessments of our lives and thereafter assign meaning or value to them. Jameson wrote that in the postmodern we experience incredulity toward the metanarrative. This implies to some extent that perhaps the metanarrative still exists, but that nobody is willing or able to believe it. It is possible that the metanarrative exists yet we collectively and individually have not the care or thought to commit. Perhaps we simply don't have the motivation to invest, or to seek.

In the past we've had the world religions for moral and spiritual guidance. Today individuals have enough information to inform them of all the wars and endless controversy religions have caused. Where do individuals turn for this moral and spiritual guidance? In the past we've had the community leaders,

G. O'Toole, *Sustainable Web Ecosystem Design*,
SpringerBriefs in Computer Science, DOI: 10.1007/978-1-4614-7714-3_18,
© The Author(s) 2013

politicians, and maybe even business executives to offer political and economic advisement. Today are bombarded daily with stories breaking of these so-called leaders' who seem to spend more time defending themselves from fraudulent and other illegal charges than they do being leaders. In this type of environment whom can individuals trust? These are some of the metanarratives that individuals once had as a resource on how to get by and how to live happily. Now, in our dominantly information-based age individuals see the emphasis on the self and often times it can feel as though the only metanarrative that individuals are offered on a mass scale is consumerism. When a daily avalanche of consumerist messages point audiences toward consumption as the way to happiness, it becomes increasingly difficult to sort through the content and find real significance, after all, it seems that individuals are unable even to agree on what really matters.

Media consumers find themselves floating around in the informational ecosystem taking in and trying to digest all of this information. We try to know what Fox News says are the facts, and what CNN posts on their Web site as the important news, but a major issue is the angles that they as the producers of information choose to take. That is, the words they use, their terminology, their attitudes, in short, the perspective from which they chose to tell the story. For example: Considering the conditions in the Middle East, a major news network was found to use the word "terrorist" when talking about the deaths caused by Palestinian militants. When talking about the deaths caused by Israel militants the same network used words (i.e. euphemisms) such as "fighters," "soldiers," and "army" and chose not to use the word "terrorist". This creates an interesting conflict for sure.

When news organizations carry out their duties to inform the public in this conflicting way, basically they are skewing the data about which they are supposed to be reporting objectively. This is a problem. It is for these and other reasons that the questions individuals need to ask is why are they doing this? Is it for their own interests? What is are the motivations for taking these positions? Are they being influenced by national hegemony?

These are important issues in considering our place in the information age and the delicate balance of information production, dissemination, and consumption. Considering these ideas of Jameson's is an important part of mapping the anatomy of sustainable Web ecosystem design.

Suggested Reading(s):
Jameson, Frederic: "Postmodernism or, the Cultural Logic of Late Capitalism"
Professor Jameson's Bibliography at Duke University:
http://fds.duke.edu/db/aas/Romance/faculty/jameson/publications

18.2 Jean Francois Lyotard

Jean Francois Lyotard, on the other hand, has completely "eradicated" the metanarrative all together. No matter if we have the motivation to seek, and the will to locate, in the end the grand narrative is not there to be found. Considering these ideas of Lyotard's is an important part of mapping the anatomy of sustainable Web ecosystem design.

In his book "The Postmodern Condition" Lyotard shows that the scientific metadiscourse has been legitimated by appealing to metanarratives or grand narratives. In this sense the metanarrative is a characteristically modern phenomenon. Throughout history tribal and premodern people have told stories that tell a grand story, however metanarratives are stories that not only tell a grand story, but also claim to be able to legitimate or prove the story's claim by an appeal to universal reason (Smith). While the metanarrative has been legitimated with an appeal to science and reason, "the scientific discourse has been propelled by the grand narrative of progress, whether by progressive political emancipation or the progressive accumulation of systematized knowledge" (Smith). This renders the metanarrative as no more legitimate than any other narrative. In this sense the metanarrative "fails to do what modern theorists wanted it to do: provide external verification for one's beliefs" (Smith). Lyotard's definition of postmodern as incredulity towards metanarratives is an explanation of these ways in which the metanarrative is loosing its credibility.

As Lyotard writes in The Postmodern Condition, information has lost its use-value. In times past, concerning points of culture, there was a certain knowledge commodity that evolved from the work, for example, that a writer created or contributed to the greater good. This knowledge came in the creative form of authentic contributory elements: a page of prose, a poem, or a novel. This contribution constituted by the unique knowledge of the writer was the end in itself. A genuine work of art was the reason for doing the work of art. In the postmodern this is lost. The information that constitutes knowledge has taken on the new role of value, or the form of value. The producers and consumers of information are much like the producers and consumers of commodities, which is to say they are separate from that which they produce or consume and they take part in that which they produce or consume only for exchange. "Knowledge ceases to be an end in itself, it loses its use-value" (Lyotard).

Lyotard writes that metanarratives legitimate, but he also writes that the metanarrative has been eradicated from Western culture and that efficiency (i.e. a fast-track to profit) is the only model left (Lyotard). What does this mean for legitimation?

The role or value of knowledge has changed. Prior to the changes brought on during the twentieth century there was the idea that as a person grew as a person, got older, did more, this individual gained a knowledge that added to the process and made life more significant, more meaningful. This idea, in itself to some extent, was a good reason to live and prosper: a key characteristic of modernity.

The change Lyotard notes is that now, knowledge (experiential understanding, scientifically learned truth, research, teaching and learning) takes on a different sort of role, or has a different type of value. It is no longer the end in itself, but a means to a different end (personal, financial gain) because it (or information) can be bought and sold as a commodity. Looking at the vast array of products and services on the market today, it can be seen that every commodity, every product, almost every service, on some level is information: a key characteristic of post-modernity. Lyotard points out accurately that today we have a significant break between people and their knowledge. Knowledge has become a commodity; technological growth in the open market has made it possible.

Lyotard clarifies the changing meaning and use of the idea of knowledge. These changes are due largely to economic factors. He holds that knowledge is changing from something a person used to earn as part of the human growth process (German phrase is Bildung), to something much more like a commodity, the atomic element to the open market system. It is known from Karl Marx that the commodity is the basic building block of capitalism. In the capitalist system people don't relate to people necessarily, but that people's commodities (their goods and services which they are building, buying, making, or selling) relate to other people's goods and services (Marx). Commodities have value which is made up of two kinds of value: use value: the horse that plows a farmer's field, and exchange value: the potatoes a farmer harvests which can be traded for flour with his neighbor. Lyotard states that increasingly now, there is this break between people and their knowledge, because knowledge is turning into something that only has a value because it can be bought and sold. From Lyotard:

> We may expect a thorough exteriorization of knowledge with respect to the knower, at whatever point he or she may occupy in the knowledge process. The old principle that the acquisition of knowledge is in dissociable (or inseparable) from the training (Bildung) of minds, or even of individuals, is becoming obsolete and will become ever more so. The relationship of the suppliers and individuals of knowledge to the knowledge they supply and use is now tending, and will increasingly tend, to assume the form already taken by the relationship of commodity producers and consumers to the commodities they produce and consume – that is, the form of value. Knowledge is and will be produced in order to be sold, it is and will be consumed in order to be valorized in a new production: in both cases, the goal is exchange. Knowledge ceases to be an end in itself: it looses its use-value. (Lyotard)

In "The Rise of the Network Society" Manuel Castells illustrates a clear ana-lytical distinction between the terms "informational society" and "information society" that is supportive of Lyotard's established loss of use-value for knowl-edge. In the cultural context, information society implies a culture based around scholasticism. Societies as far back to medieval Europe and beyond attributed a great sense of value to this type of cultural intellectual framework. What sets an "informational society" apart from this type of society is the historical change that causes a rewrite of the role of information. With new technological conditions in place, "information generation, processing, and transmission become the funda-mental sources of productivity and power" (Castells 21). The current informational condition is not simply a world where there is information, but a world where "the social and technological forms of industrial organization permeate all spheres of activity, starting with the dominant activities, located in the economic system and in military technology, and reaching the objects and habits of everyday life" (Castells 21).

The direct causes of these changes in the role of information are very hard to get at. There seems to be little concrete proof of as of yet. Lyotard writes that models are legitimated by certain narratives—that narratives legitimate. And to make the situation more complex, since the end of WWII, the narratives people used to use as guides in life, in making decisions, in putting meaning to things, have been eradicated. Further, performativity has all but replaced the meta-narrative. The downside of which is that all performativity cares about is efficiency in the give and take and seems not to be concerned at all about ethical matters. There is a positivist philosophy of efficiency (Lyotard) that puts faith in the stability of performativity. But what if it is not? The process can be witnessed across not only the Western world but the Far East as well of change from local involvement in one's church, as an example, to conditions and structures that more closely align with the intended efficiency of big business.

As a further example, under such conditions it is understandable to think that since 2007, one might have a bit less faith in sheer performativity of the open market system that comprises the United States. It was during this time that The Great Recession, as it has been called, in the U.S. began as a direct result of the over extension of an economic culture of unstable "default swops", derivatives—a method of commodifying loan risk—subprime mortgages, and other toxic assets being sold to unsuspecting investors by many large banks in the U.S. collectively referred to as Wall Street. The buyers of these bad investments were individuals, businesses, banks, and municipalities both domestic and abroad. The reach of the sales was far and wide, as was the eventual destruction that the investments caused. Perhaps these financiers assumed a positivist approach and considered their acts to be innovative. Perhaps they believed they were creative and had invented a new, profitable, harmless commodity, one that was not only efficient, but lustfully profitable. As history clearly teaches, in reality the opaque if not deceptive culture and practice of these banks, their leaders, and their traders caused unprecedented damage as "the housing bubble (in the U.S.) burst and trillions of dollars' worth of toxic mortgages began to go bad in 2007, fear spread through the massive firms that form the heart of Wall Street. By the spring of 2008, burdened by billions of dollars of bad mortgages," megabanks Bear Stearns, Fannie Mae, Freddie Mac, Lehman Brothers, and many other institutions large and small failed and declared bankruptcy ("Inside the Meltdown").

In a condition such as this, when performativity has substituted for the meta-narrative and performativity alone has so much potential for failure the question of legitimation naturally arises. Who legitimates? What do they legitimate? Who gives them the right to legitimate? Who follows? For what reasons? For these questions it is of utmost importance to look at this relationship between narrative knowledge, meaning, and legitimation to attempt to more fully understand the

direct correlation between these concepts and what the workflow is therein. It is
the hypothesis of this work that the percentage of narrative knowledge constituting
these social bonds is in a state of flux due in large part to the ubiquitous use of
contemporary communication media technology and it's invention of the "active
audience" (which is discussed further in the next chapter). This change in the
percentage of narrative knowledge in the social bonds of self, medium, and
environment, coupled with the loss of the legitimating metanarrative has created a
curious type of void, this time, concerning legitimation. The next chapter discusses
the process of media influencing the information consumer by piecing together the
ideas of Viktor Frankl, Eric Hoffer, Karl Marx, Theodore Adorno, Jean-Francois
Lyotard, and others and discovers that under such an ambiguous set of conditions
the need for a critical filter in media and information consumption is established.
The chapter concludes with the idea that, at least since the time of Lyotard's
eradication of the metanarrative, the critical filter at use within the individual is
necessary as a method of maintaining legitimation in the postmodern: or a type of
post-legitimation.

Suggested Book(s):
Lyotard, Jean Francois: "The Postmodern Condition"
Castells, Manuel: "The Rise of Networked Society"

18.3 Harold Innis

Canadian scholar Harold Innis knew that the university as a culturally beneficial
and intellectually necessary environment was not perfect, in fact, far from it. He
devoted much of his life to establishing and improving the higher education system
of Canada. Among Harold Innis' many contributions was the clarification of an
attribute of sociocultural evolution. Innis wrote that borrowing from the cultural
context of the past toward the cultural context of the new must inherently be a
highly selective process. The reason for Innis' selectivity is simply to avoid an
over abundance of unneeded cultural baggage. This idea or process in itself provides certain constructive if not obvious benefits. The amassment of just about
anything without a proper civilizing filter in place in order to avoid overload
certainly carries its burdens. But Innis went further in his reasoning and included
that there was more pretext for this exacting process. Importantly, this operation of
purposely and consciously leaving behind certain sociocultural cargo will logis-
tically leave a conditional void or a type of intellectual incompleteness. To Innis
this is necessary so that there is continually a culturally perceived need for new
ideas, and so that there is room for them to enter and flourish. Without this
necessary incompleteness, the sense of a demand or requisite for new ideas and
innovation is aborted as well as the possibility of creating a positive environment

for active "continuous discussion of vital problems" (Innis). Innis came to the conclusion that it is an effect of modern mediated communication technology, with its ever-increasing attribute of flawless efficiency and quantity of content (the cultural baggage), that rather senselessly and somewhat automatically fills this void and, in a sense, renders the incomplete complete, but in an insignificant way; that the modern forces of media communication technology harness a "continuous, systematic, ruthless destruction of elements of permanence essential to cultural activity" (Innis 11). For Innis this was a great crisis for the West, and a sign of its eventual downfall.

A central element to the lifelong project of Harold Innis concerns the progress of Western Civilization and posits that intellectual contributions must come from the periphery of a civilization, and that those contributions then become part of the new "centre for cultural florescence" (Watson). This condition is a requirement for a civilization's renewal. It is clear in the work of Innis that two entities are at play in any successful civilization: power and intelligence, or force and knowledge, politics and scholarship. Specific institutions are needed in order to pursue both because they cannot be pursued in unison. Power, force, politics is manifest in the military, local police, courts of law, the bureaucracy, the automated workplace. Simultaneously, intelligence, knowledge, scholarship is found mainly in the university. The former have their reason for being and main functions served in the "transmission of orders, obedience, and an absence of potentially contestatory thinking" (Watson). The latter thrives and flourishes with the academic freedom of educational systems that should be protected from political and financial outside influence. For Innis the conflict inherent places power as bête noire to intelligence.

> The Industrial Revolution and the mechanized knowledge have all but destroyed the scholar's influence. Force is no longer concerned with his protection and is actively engaged in schemes for his destruction. Enormous improvements in communication have made understanding more difficult. Even science, mathematics, and music as the last refuge of Western mind have come under the spell of the mechanized vernacular. (Innis)

Alexander John Watson notes that, in regard to what Innis gained from his time at The University of Chicago, that

> Innis took from the Chicago School (of Social Thought) the view that while genuine but incremental advances in knowledge could be made using the perspective implicit in an existing paradigm, the really significant advances in knowledge took place when these older paradigms were confronted with new general perspectives emanating from previously marginalized social groups. (Watson 121)

The life expectancy of an empire is affected directly by the dominant media effecting that civilization. The comparative lifespan, weight, strength and durability of the particular medium in question "virtually determines the make-up of the corresponding empire" (Watson 314). Innis' research aligns heavier media, such as stone or clay tablets, which are dominant in the communication of an empire, with other characteristics of that empire such as a bias toward time, duration, the oral tradition, and continuity. On the other side of the coin, there are empires with a predominant use of non-durable media such as papyrus, paper, and electronic formats which are aligned with characteristics such as expansion, a bias toward space, discontinuity, a written tradition, armed force and a secular military government. Innis stressed that the success of an imperial project is dependent on a balance of various media that fall on each of these two sides in order that they complement one another for the duration of the project.

The destruction of an empire is due directly to the imbalanced relationship discussed above, of power and intelligence, which are the two necessary meta-elements to a successful civilization. Among a body of significant work in the study of classics and investigations on intelligence and power throughout history, Eric Havelock concludes with "the sheer will to control and order and compel is itself a historical force in human society and in the human soul working in constant antagonism to intelligence which it distrusts and despises and crucifies" (Havelock). "Havelock summarizes ... the dilemma of modern man as 'the conflict of intelligence and power" (Watson 305) toward the collapse of Western civilization.

A significant contribution, perhaps the highest of which, from Harold Innis, is his analysis of a combinatory nature of a theory of communication media, a theory of empire, and a theory of human consciousness. This contribution from Innis has been partially overlooked as a result of the context from which it has been examined. A great deal of those scholars who have done the overlooking tend to be political scientists who are interested in the earlier economic work of Innis, mainly having to do with the staples deterministic approach to Canada's economic development. This inclusion of the consciousness element, in such cases, is not only seen as one of "softness" in comparison to the "hardness" to the field of political economics, but also a branch of Innis' work that has over reached its scientific jurisdiction. Additionally, it has been critiqued that, with a well established background in economics as opposed to psychology, Innis felt more at home with dealing with the institutional and the technological nodes of this approach to examining change and affect. In his last ten years, Innis moved steadily toward a concern for human consciousness as a key element in the relationships of power and communications in the development of the Western world (Watson 324).

Innis built his analysis of empire by employing the uses of dominant media communications technologies within those civilizations and analyzing the dominant characteristics of the media in use. He found that civilizations that use more permanent media have a bias of time domination. Civilizations that use less permanent media have a bias for space domination. It is central to Innis' work that these primary concepts, space and time, in the context of imperial dynamics, can be restructured and controlled by the directing groups of a society.

> Innis' terms 'monopoly of information' and 'monopoly of force' refer to the institutional formations within a polity that appropriate for themselves the right to construct the way in which time and space are perceived by ordinary members of the society. (Watson 328)

To examine this idea reveals a thorough contradiction to what Innis says is necessary for the advancement and success of an imperial project: voices or input from the margins, that is, innovative and creative thought which cannot come from a self-referencing center of empire. This idea was so central to Innis' ideas that he included it in speeches he gave in 1949 to a graduate colloquium to the effect of "students should be brought to the precipice, beyond which knowledge does not exist" (Innis Papers). For the directing groups of a society to manipulate these concepts of time and space for their subjects, is for these directing groups to believe that time and space are fixed entities, the contents for which need to be continually articulated at an ever more convincing pace. For example, an organized institution such as the Christian church is backed by the particular media communication technology of parchment. This institution has a certain amount of power over its subjects and retains that power by "formulating a particular conception of time" (Watson 328). It is a monopoly for two reasons: 1. The rules and information are created and disseminated by a relatively small group of rulers; and 2. These ideas come to dominate the vernacular of the era so much so that the prospects of any other potentially competitive institution with another concept of time is kept from gaining ground, at least temporarily. However, this requires work and effort in continually articulating the church's concept of time, a further burden on the power entity that uses up its resources and opens itself up to competition. The power entity becomes caught within a self-referencing system of thought and progress.

Although Innis was not greatly concerned with the individual as much as the collective conscious, the importance of a sense of incompleteness from the past to the present cultural milieu may be applied to the individual as well as a society. For Innis embarking on an experiment of the individual consciousness would have been redundant due to his position and tendency to "equate institutional dynamics with the sum total of activities of the individuals association with the institution" (Watson). Considering these ideas of Innis' is an important part of mapping the anatomy of sustainable Web ecosystem design.

Suggested Book(s):
Innis, Harold: "Empire and Communications"

18.4 Emile Durkheim

If cultural sociologist Emile Durkheim is correct, CNN an any number of other sources of mediated information have the potential abilities to inform the general public on how to live, on how to understand, and in what ways they may be successful in their pursuit of happiness. According to Durkheim, this collective representation followed by a mediated identity-forming process informs us of what to wear, what to eat, how to speak, how to spend the time, how to spend the money, and even what to believe is important. From birth individuals are enmeshed within a "whole system of representations by means of which men understand each other" (Durkheim). And if, time after time, individuals are told by

CNN, MSNBC, Fox, HBO, Hollywood, NBC, and People.com what it is individuals need to know, and—according to these producers of media content—how individuals are to feel about what individuals are being told, does this not influence the consumers' daily lives? Kinder and Iyengar show that media "news shapes the relative importance Americans attach to various national problems" and that media outlets for news "powerfully influence which problems we regard as the nation's most serious." The question then must be asked: Can the same affective empowerment be attributed to the advertisements these media outlets run? Considering these ideas of Durkheim's and other sociologists and philosophers of technology is an important part of mapping the anatomy of sustainable Web ecosystem design.

Suggested Reading(s):

Durkheim, Emile. *The Division of Labour in Society*

Chapter 19
Conclusion

The Web must be maintained in a way that supports and encourages creative and innovative heights to human progress. Among all of the other ideas discussed in this book, you may even consider it the meta-idea, innovation stands out. You may want your work to stand out in a world where there are potentially billions of other options for your users. Innovation is a necessary node that must be considered when mapping the anatomy of sustainable Web ecosystem design. Innovation not only maps back to just about every section of this book, but this book itself is essentially an example of innovation. Sure, you can find all kinds of instructional documentation online that will explain what a jpg is used for, or what an SQL injection can do to a Web site, but what is innovative here is how all of these nodes, including humans, work together to form a new ecosystem, a cyborg ecosystem, that, for the most part, we can control. The astounding part of this all is the change that this ecosystem is bringing to our lives; the effect is has on our reality, and what it means to be human. Innovation is having an understanding of the fundamentals of a product or field, and then bringing creative perspectives, ideas, and uses to that field. The Web itself is probably the most significant single innovation on humanity in the past century. It is important to know how to recognize innovation, and how to achieve a bit of your own innovation. It is certainly easier said than done, and innovation must be sustained for the duration of the lifespan of the project, not just during planning and development stages.

In conclusion, we have to remember that this is a theory, a methodology as well as a development model. It is difficult to put what we are talking about and working on here into a neat and clean box. We know that is the case because what we are really talking about here is organizing, indexing, and making it fun to access information. As we know, information is everything, everywhere, all of the time. That is tough to get your head around let alone to become its master manipulator. Everything mentioned in this book is important as an early road map to understanding the necessary nodes that must be considered when working with the anatomy of sustainable Web ecosystem design. This map will change as time progresses. The most important thing is to be mindful of these coming changes.

G. O'Toole, *Sustainable Web Ecosystem Design*,
SpringerBriefs in Computer Science, DOI: 10.1007/978-1-4614-7714-3_19,
© The Author(s) 2013

Book Editions/Versioning Information

This is the first edition of this book. It is being released in a sort of beta format to work out any bugs, typos, or miscommunications by critical mass and by clear intent of the author. Updates and revisions will be made in future editions of the book. Please send all feedback to the author, Greg O'Toole by email to gto1@psu.edu.

G. O'Toole, *Sustainable Web Ecosystem Design*,
SpringerBriefs in Computer Science, DOI: 10.1007/978-1-4614-7714-3,
© The Author(s) 2013

References

This reference list adheres to the MLA 7ᵗʰ (6ᵗʰ for footnotes) Edition style

Alcott, Blake. "Jevon's Paradox." *Ecological Economics*. 54.1 (2005): 9-21. Print.

Barthes, Roland. *Image, Music, Text*. 77. New York: Hill and Wang, 1978. Print.

Baumann, Nicole, and Danielle Pham-Dinh. "Biology of Oligodendrocyte and Myelin in the Mammalian Central Nervous System." Physiological Review. 81.2 (2001): 871-927. Web. 22 Dec. 2012. http://physrev.physiology.org/content/81/2/871.long.

Benedikt, Michael, Juliana Freire, and Godefroid Patrice. "VeriWeb: Automatically Testing Dynamic Web Sites." *Bell Laboratories, Lucent Technologies*. n. page. Web. 18 Dec. 2012. http://www2002.org/CDROM/alternate/654/.

Berners-Lee, T. & Cailliau, R. (1990). WorldWideWeb: proposal for a hypertext project. World Wide Web Consortium, (Massachusetts Institute of Technology, Institut National de Recherche en Informatique et en Automatique, Keio University). Retrieved Dec 20, 2012 from http://www.w3.org/Proposal.html

Castells, Manuel. *The Rise of the Network Society (The Information Age: Economy, Society and Culture)*. 2. Vol. 1. Oxford: Wiley-Blackwell Publishing, 2000. Print.

Chenet, S.K. et al., Hematopoietic origin of pathological grooming in Hoxb8 mutant mice. Cell 141, 775 (2010).

Craib, Alice, Perry, Margaret. *EEG Handbook*, 2nd Edition. Beckman, 1975.

Dolman, C.L. *Textbook of Neuropathology*, R. L. Davis, D. M. Robertson, Eds. (Williams & Wilkins, Baltimore, MD, 1991), pp. 141–163.

Durkheim, Emile. *The Division of Labour in Society*. Free Press, 1997. Print.

Field, Douglas. "Glia: The new frontier in brain science." *Guest Blog*. Scientific American, 04 2010. Web. Web. 22 Dec. 2012. http://blogs.scientificamerican.com/guest-blog/2010/11/04/glia-the-new-frontier-in-brain-science/.

Field, Douglas. Interview by Leonard Lopate. "The Other Brain." *The Leonard Lopate Show*. 22 Jan 2010. WNYC, New York. Radio. http://www.wnyc.org/shows/lopate/2010/jan/22/the-other-brain/.

"glia". Oxford Dictionaries. April 2010. Oxford Dictionaries. April 2010. Oxford University Press. 22 December 2012. http://oxforddictionaries.com/definition/english/glia?q=glia.

Graeber, Manuel B. "Changing Face of Microglia." Science. 330.6005 (2010): 783-788. Web. 22 Dec. 2012.

Guest Contributor. "Information taxonomy plays a critical role in Web site design and search processes." *TechRepublic*. 01 2003: n. page. Web. 2 Jan. 2013. http://www.techrepublic.com/article/information-taxonomy-plays-a-critical-role-in-web-site-design-and-search-processes/5054221.

G. O'Toole, *Sustainable Web Ecosystem Design*,
SpringerBriefs in Computer Science, DOI: 10.1007/978-1-4614-7714-3,
© The Author(s) 2013

Hanson, Fergus. "Internet Freedom: The Role of the U.S. State Department." *Brookings*. Brookings Institute, 25 2012. Web. 31 Dec 2012. http://www.brookings.edu/research/reports/2012/10/25-ediplomacy-hanson-internet-freedom.

Havelock, E.A. *Prometheus Bound The Crucifixion of Intellectual Man*, Boston Beacon, 1950. Print.

Innis, Harold. *Changing Concepts of Time*. New York: Rowman and Littlefield, 2004. eBook.

Innis, Harold. *Empire and Communications*. Oxford: Clarendon Press, 1950. Print.

Innis, Harold. Speech to Graduate Colloquium [1949], Innis Papers, University of Toronto Archives.

Innis, Harold. *The Bias of Communication*. Toronto: University of Toronto Press, Scholarly Publishing Division, 1999. Print.

Institute of Electrical and Electronics Engineers. IEEE Standard Computer Dictionary: A Compilation of IEEE Standard Computer Glossaries. New York, NY: 1990.

"Internet Usage Statistics." *Internet World Stats*. Miniwatts Marketing Group, June 30 2012. Web. 5 Dec 2012. http://www.internetworldstats.com/stats.htm.

Interoperable, Wikipedia Entry, Last retrieved 28 Dec 2012.

Iyengar, S., and D.M. Kinder. *News That Matters*. Chicago: University of Chicago Press, 1987. Print.

Jameson, Frederic. "Postmodernism or, the Cultural Logic of Late Capitalism." Media and cultural studies key works. Ed. Meenakshi Giri Durham and Douglas M. Kellner. UK: Blackwell publishing, 2001. 550-587.

Kittler, Friedrich. "Die Laterna magica der Literatur: Schillers und Hoffmanns Medienstrategien." *Athenaum: Jahrbuch fur Romantik*. (1994): 219. Print.

Kirk, Michael, prod. "Inside the Meltdown." *Frontline*. PBS: 02 February 2009. Television. http://www.pbs.org/wgbh/pages/frontline/view/.

Linder, Douglas, O. "Famous American Trials The O.J. Simpson Trial 1995." University of Missouri-Kansas City. College of Law, n.d. Web. 24 December 2010. http://www.law.umkc.edu/faculty/projects/ftrials/simpson/simpson.htm.

Le Hégaret, Philippe Le. "Document Object Model." *World Wide Web Consortium*. W3C, 01 2009. Web. 28 Dec 2012. http://www.w3.org/DOM/#what.

Marcotte, Ethan. *Responsive Web Design*. A Book Apart, 2012. Print.

Markiewicz, Peter. "Save the planet through sustainable web design." *.Net Magazine*. 17 2012: n. page. Web. 29 Dec. 2012. http://www.netmagazine.com/features/save-planet-through-sustainable-web-design.

Morville, Peter. *Ambient Findability, What We Find Changes Who We Become*. O'Reilly Media, 2005. Print.

"neuroglia, n.". OED Online. December 2012. Oxford University Press. 22 December 2012. http://www.oed.com.ezaccess.libraries.psu.edu/view/Entry/126393.

Pentti Malaska and Matti Vapaavuori, eds. *The Club of Rome "The Dossiers" 1965-1984*. 15 September 2005. Vienna: Finnish Association for the Club of Rome (FICOR), 2005. 62. Print.

Smith, James. *Who's Afraid of Postmodernism? Taking Derrida, Lyotard, and Foucault to Church*. Baker Publishing Group, 2006. Web.

Sounders, Steve. "The Performance Golden Rule." *SteveSounders.com*. Google, 10 2012. Web. 29 Dec 2012. http://www.stevesouders.com/blog/2012/02/10/the-performance-golden-rule/.

U.S Department of Commerce. "A Look Ahead to 2012: NTIA by the Numbers." United States Department of Commerce. United States Government, 30 2011. Web. 29 Dec 2012. http://www.commerce.gov/blog/2011/12/30/look-ahead-2012-ntia-numbers.

Watson, Alexander John. *Marginal Man: The Dark Vision of Harold Innis*. Toronto: University of Toronto Press, 2006. Print.

Wheeler, John Archibald. Recent Thinking about the Nature of the Physical World: It from Bit. *Annals of the New York Academy of Sciences* 655.1 frontiers in 01 Jun 1992: 349-364. New York Academy of Sciences. 18 Dec 2012.

Wroblewski, Luke. Mobile First. A Book Apart, 2012. Print.

W3C Schools. "Browser Statistics and Trends." *W3C Schools*. W3C Schools, n.d. Web. 20 Dec 2012. http://www.w3schools.com/browsers/browsers_stats.asp.

Yuhas, Daisy, and Ferris Jabr. "Know Your Neurons: Meet the Glia." *Brainwaves*. Scientific American, 18 2012. Web. Web. 22 Dec. 2012. http://blogs.scientificamerican.com/brainwaves/2012/05/18/know-your-neurons-meet-the-glia/.